GETTING THROUGH

A Systematic Approach To Being Understood

By Ed Paulson, PhD, MBA

Pro Chango

Publishing   Consulting   Learning

La Grange, IL USA

Getting Through: A Systematic Approach To Being Understood
Copyright © 2023 by Edward Paulson.

Outcome Oriented Communication is a trademark of Edward Paulson.
Paulson Media Matching Method is a trademark of Edward Paulson.

Paperback ISBN: 979-8-9879508-0-7
Kindle ISBN: 979-8-9879508-1-4
Library of Congress Control Number: 2023906185

Printed in the *United States of America*.

Technical edited by: Laura Pesek
Copy edited by: Alexander Rose
Layout design for print, E-book, and Kindle versions by: Saheran Shoukat
Cover design and art by: Saheran Shoukat
Illustrations by: Edward Paulson

First paperback edition.

To request permission, contact the publisher at author@edpaulson.com. Subject Line: Getting Through Permission Request

ProChango LLC, 121 West Hillgrove Ave., #220, La Grange, IL 60525 USA, www.edpaulson.com

Acknowledgments

There are many who contributed to the approach described in this book and who helped make its publication possible. I want to thank Charles Perrow, Richard Daft, and Robert Lengel for their insightful research that first prompted my interest in media richness theory, task routineness, and organizational communication as a science. Thank you to Reuben McDaniel, the professor who included this new (at the time) media richness theory approach to communication in his human resources class. Thanks go to Laura Pesek for being a true believer in the value of this approach and for technically reviewing the draft. Her wealth of experience was often a reality check for applying and explaining the concepts. Thank you to Dan McManus, president of TeamFloral, for his willingness to learn about and apply the approach operationally. Thank you, Penny Giza, for your second technical review. My appreciation goes to the scores of people with whom I have worked over the past decades who taught me what did and did not work when interacting with customers, projects, people, the media, and each other. I hope you know who you are.

I want to thank the hundreds of working adult students who have taken my communication courses and provided helpful feedback about how this approach has worked in their workplaces. Their continued encouragement to "get this book out there" kept me writing, believing that what is presented can help improve communication, which is deeply needed in today's fractured world. I want to thank my family for supporting me as I locked myself in the office working on "the book" and my friends for patiently listening to me talk about how excited I was to find another example of how the concepts worked.

Finally, I want to thank you, the readers, for trusting me enough to invest your time and money into learning this communication approach. Without you, none of this would be possible. I sincerely hope that you reach out to me and let me know your thoughts. As you will see, only through feedback can we improve how we communicate to ensure that we are fully understood as intended.

About the Author

Ed Paulson is the author of over 15 published books through respected publishing houses such as John Wiley and Sons, Inc. and Alpha Books/ Macmillan. His most famous book is "The Complete Idiot's Guide to Starting Your Own Business," which has sold over 200,000 copies and remains one of the bestselling entrepreneurship books ever published. Dr. Paulson has been a member of the DePaul University faculty since 2001, developing and teaching courses in organizational communication, entrepreneurship, business management, risk management, financial analysis, and research. Ed is included in the prestigious Marquis Who's Who edition.

He has been in professional communication for over 40 years, working in sales, marketing, national account, engineering, public relations, and general management positions in Silicon Valley, Austin, and Chicago. Through ProChango he offers his experience to leaders through books, business consulting, leadership coaching, and seminars. His goal has been and remains to be of service to others with the goal of helping them and their organizations succeed.

Ed can be contacted through his website, www.edpaulson.com, E-mail at author@edpaulson.com, on LinkedIn at www.linkedin.com/in/etpaulson, and on Facebook at www.facebook.com/EdPaulsonAuthor. Reach out to Ed to see how you can put his experience to work helping you create your successes!

Dedication

This book is dedicated to all of us who struggle to be understood.

Tell Us What You Think!

You are the reason that this book was written, and your feedback is appreciated in ways in which this book or other ProChango titles can be improved. We would appreciate you taking a few minutes to let us know what we are doing right, where we can improve, topics that you would like to see us publish, and anything else you want to pass along. Thank you for purchasing this book, and we hope that you consider other ProChango titles.

You can contact us in a few ways;

Email: author@edpaulson.com

Phone: 630-960-3299

Snail Mail: Reader Feedback, ProChango LLC, 121 West Hillgrove Ave., #220, La Grange, IL 60525 USA

Table of Contents

Introduction
Is This Book For You?

The fact that you are reading this right now indicates to me that you have more than a casual interest in becoming a better communicator. Nice! It has been shown time and again that those viewed as better communicators are more likely to be successful in getting others to follow them.

If you are someone who manages or supervises others, this book is for you. If you are someone who needs to manage upward in your organization to your bosses and their bosses, this book is for you. If you have ever wondered whether to send an email, pick up the phone or have a meeting and really had no idea how to make that decision, this book is for you. If you have ever felt like the person you are talking to would rather be doing something else other than talking to you, this book is for you. If you find that your emails, voice messages, and invitations are being ignored, this book is for you. If you are a leader that feels like those you lead are not going in the direction you intend, this book is for you. If you are a manager whose team is underperforming, this book is for you. If you are in sales, marketing, or customer service and have difficult customers, no matter what you try to do for them, this book is for you. If you are frustrated with the way communication in your organization works (or doesn't work), this book is for you.

This book is intended to make you a better business communicator. So, if you and your significant other are having problems talking about money or raising your family, this book is probably not right for you. If you are looking for guidance on how to best talk to your teenage daughter about dating, this book is probably not right for you. (Not sure anyone knows how to do that!) Some of the concepts might be applicable to personal situations, but that is not the focus of this book.

There are three books in this core series. Book One, "Getting Through: A Systematic Approach to Being Understood" (this book), offers a framework for matching communication media, such as email, text, telephone, or a meeting, to the requirements of a particular communication situation, a little understood yet very important consideration. The Second Book, "Getting Agreement: Designing Messages That Create Cooperation," offers a systematic approach to gaining the cooperation of others by designing the right message for the right people that is then reliably delivered using the Book One approach. The Third Book in the core series "Flexibly Tough: Building Resilient Organizations Using Communication" provides a systematic approach for managers to use when designing their organization's structure based on personnel, required tasks, operational flow, information, and the communication foundation needed to tie it all together for successful task completion. The concepts in Book One and Book Two are integral to understanding the approach offered in Book Three.

My thinking behind this approach is simple. The most immediate daily need we have is selecting the proper media for a communication situation to ensure that your delivered message is understood by your audience as intended. After completing the First Book, you will have a deeper appreciation for the importance of the message, which leads us to Book Two, where you will learn ways to evaluate a problem to determine your constraints and desired outcomes, learn how people make decisions, and investigate ways of influencing others so that they are more likely to cooperate with you. All this leads to developing a message that, when properly delivered using the concepts in Book One, will get you your desired outcome. These two books together offer you powerful tools for enhancing your success as a communicator and leader. Book Three is for managers who are looking to improve group performance using a communication-based framework for designing operational workflows based on people, experience, tasks, and information requirements. Book Three's concepts are fairly abstract, but there are very real, applied benefits for any organization that applies them in a comprehensive manner.

Over time, there will be additional books in this series that look at how these communication concepts can be applied to specific business situations, and I value your feedback on topics and ideas that you would find most valuable. The fundamentals presented here and in the other books will put the odds of business success on your side by better ensuring that those with whom you communicate clearly understand your messages as you intended and feel motivated to cooperate.

Where This Book Is Going

Take a moment to think about the various ways in which we can communicate with others in a business environment. We have offices, conference rooms, reference documentation, written reports, telephone, email, text messaging, video conferencing, instant messaging, group meetings, major presentations, and webinars, just to name a few, with more being developed all the time. Each method of communication has its own strengths and deficiencies, and we usually only learn about these traits through trial and error. Early in your career, your boss might have told you to "Call a meeting on that one" or "Just send him an email," and over time, you likely adopted similar approaches. You might have tried something on your own, and it worked, so you kept doing it. Or even more painful, you tried something on your own, and it didn't work, and now are hesitant to experiment, choosing to always use the simplest approach like email. This isn't a systematic approach to communication and media selection. This is more like a communication hazing! How are you supposed to make effective use of the amazing technological tools at your disposal if it is all learned by trial and error? That is where this book comes in.

Selecting the proper media to use for a particular situation requires an evaluation of the complexity of the topic involved, the experience level of the involved persons, the perceived risk of the situation in the minds of the various parties, the level of certainty (uncertainty) related to the pertinent information, the political complexity of the situation, and other factors as well. You may be thinking, "Seriously?" It may sound unbelievable, but it is true! This is why people struggle to find the right media match for a situation because there is so much that should be considered, and nobody has offered them a path for proper selection – until now.

Each section of this book is designed to lead you to better understand the proper application of the *Paulson Media Matching Method*^{TM}, which encompasses the various aspects listed before.

THE PAULSON MEDIA MATCHING METHOD

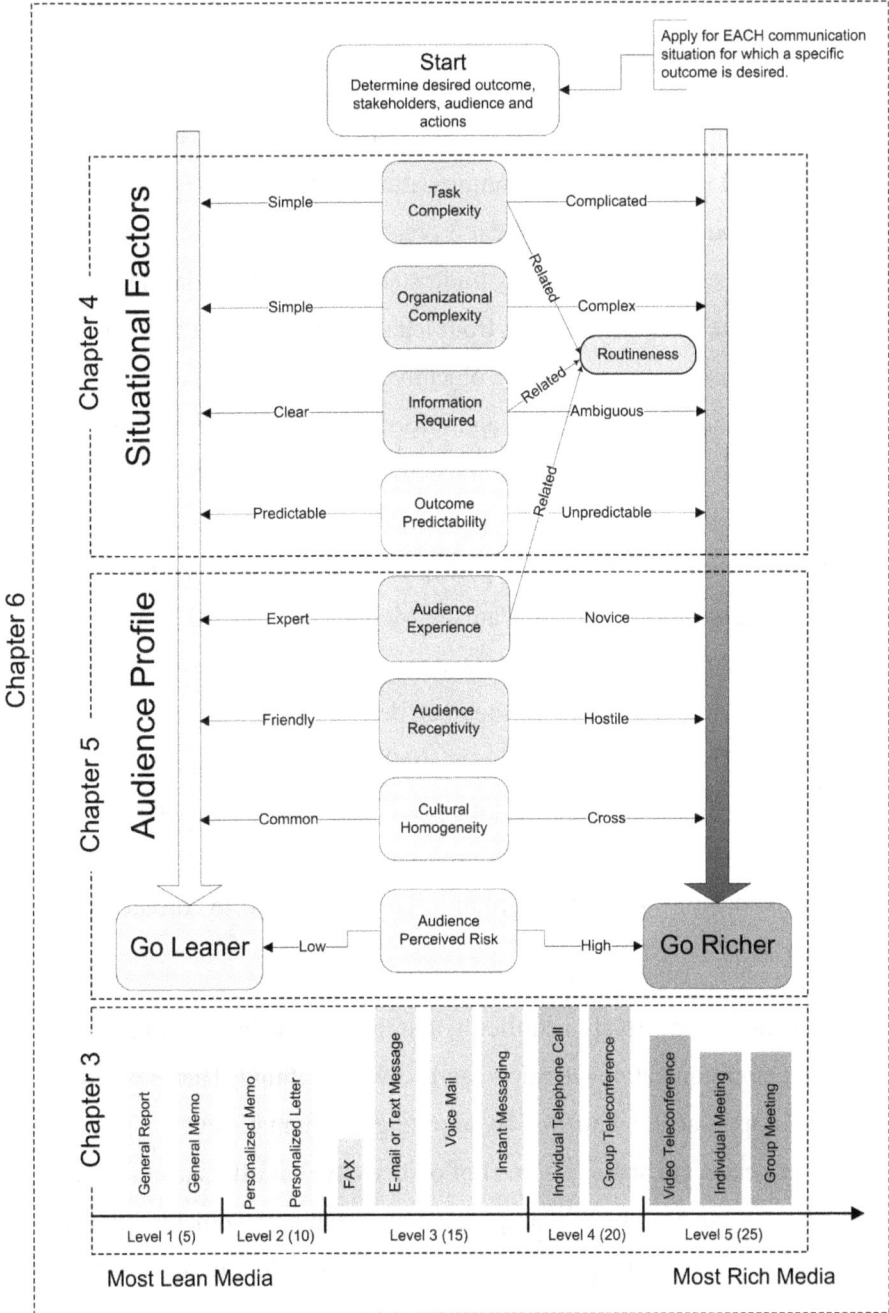

Start
Determine desired outcome, stakeholders, audience and actions

Apply for EACH communication situation for which a specific outcome is desired.

Chapter 4 — Situational Factors

Simple — **Task Complexity** — Complicated

Simple — **Organizational Complexity** — Complex

Related

Routineness

Clear — **Information Required** — Ambiguous

Related

Predictable — **Outcome Predictability** — Unpredictable

Related

Chapter 5 — Audience Profile

Expert — **Audience Experience** — Novice

Friendly — **Audience Receptivity** — Hostile

Common — **Cultural Homogeneity** — Cross

Go Leaner ← Low — **Audience Perceived Risk** — High → **Go Richer**

Chapter 3

General Report
General Memo
Personalized Memo
Personalized Letter
FAX
E-mail or Text Message
Voice Mail
Instant Messaging
Individual Telephone Call
Group Teleconference
Video Teleconference
Individual Meeting
Group Meeting

| Level 1 (5) | Level 2 (10) | Level 3 (15) | Level 4 (20) | Level 5 (25) |

Most Lean Media — Most Rich Media

Chapter 6

Different areas of the chart are grouped as topics covered in the designated chapter. For example, media richness is covered in Chapter 3, as noted by the dashed box around the various media types and richness levels at the bottom of the chart, and so forth.

The first two chapters cover some general concepts related to communication that are crucial to all forms of communication, so learning them goes far beyond this book and series. Chapter 3 presents key aspects of media richness so that readers can clearly understand what differentiates rich media, like face-to-face meetings, from lean media, such as a written report. Chapter 4 looks at the more objective influences of a communication situation, such as task complexity and information requirements. Chapter 5 looks at the more personal aspects of a communication situation, such as the experience level of the involved communicators, the culture within which they work, their attitudes, and risk perception. Chapter 6 ties it all together by presenting ways in which the Paulson Media Matching method should be used to evaluate a given communication situation to help you select the best media and richness level for message delivery. You may be tempted to skip to Chapter 6 and start applying the method on your own, but experience has shown me that skipping does not work. Folks tend to apply their own interpretations to the terms listed in the chart and incorrectly select media. Read the book (it is a short book, after all) and learn how to correctly apply the method.

Communicating effectively is difficult, and the various influences upon a particular communication situation can be overwhelming. This is where a systematic approach is valuable. By applying a systematic evaluation, we get out of our heads and achieve a level of objectivity that offers useful insight as to how we can accomplish our goals. The systems will quickly become automatic, but the world is a complex place, and should a future situation become overwhelming, you can fall back on the system to help you move forward.

It is human nature to want to be understood. This applies to both the sender and receiver of a message. You want to be understood, and your audience wants to easily and clearly understand what you are communicating. Selecting the wrong media for message delivery immediately jeopardizes the likelihood of your message being properly understood. Use the method outlined in this book to keep that from happening.

I sincerely hope that you decide to take this journey with me to understand communication as the powerful business tool that it is. Taking the time to learn the approach presented here will benefit you far into the future and become so natural that you will hardly remember a time when you did not see communication situations in this way.

In summary, if you want people to cooperate with you more frequently, this book is for you. If you want people to look forward to communicating with you, this book is for you. If you want to be better understood, this book is for you. If you want to put the odds of business success on your side, this book is for you. Let's get started.

CHAPTER ONE

Comparing Business And Personal Communication

I had an exceptional professor in MBA School who contended that businesses were simply a nexus of contracts or agreements. By this he meant that businesses were structured to obtain agreements, that the parties then acted to complete those agreements, and the agreement was complete when each party believed that their mutual and respective obligations were finished. Initially, this made a lot of sense to me, but over time I realized that this concept could be taken a step further. In their most basic form, contracts do nothing more than spell out the parties' understanding of their agreement so that those involved had a common reference related to each other's responsibilities. Contracts are communication tools. Sure, there are many different disciplines involved with creating legally binding contracts, but in the end, they are a communication tool that represents a mutual understanding, and the better each party understands the terms and conditions of the contract (agreement) the more likely the agreement is to be successfully fulfilled and the less likely to result in a contract dispute.

Everyone wins when the agreement is clear and well understood by all parties.

We often think of organizations as entities that produce some product or service that is then sold to other companies. This is only partially accurate. Without the people who work for the company, little to nothing would get accomplished. Sure, you may be representing your company but ultimately it will be one person talking to another that finalizes any business agreement.

This applies within the company as well. Every step within an organization is critical to its overall success, and coordination of the personnel between those steps is needed to move everyone toward a common goal. Coordination requires communication. This got me thinking: Could I be looking at organizations in reverse of how they really operate? Instead of looking at the organization as a manufacturer that used communication (almost as an afterthought) to get things done, perhaps I should be looking at communication FIRST with the final goal of the communication being to produce a product or service. At first this might seem like a trivial distinction, but in reality, it changes everything.

Think about the number of times that you worked to accomplish something that you felt was important, only to realize that you didn't consider how your accomplishment would impact others. Only after getting feedback, perhaps heated feedback, from others affected by your work did you then scramble to put together a communication process to explain your "accomplishment" to them. You likely made the initial changes intending to benefit others in your organization, but you put your output goal ahead communicating with those affected. If we are honest with ourselves, we should have known that at some point communication to affected parties would have to happen and considered ways of building this communication in from the beginning, but we often don't. It is astounding how often information technology departments will roll out enterprise-wide software changes and not build end user feedback and training into their development and rollout plan. How can you expect end users to react positively to a new software revision if they don't know why the change is being forced on them and don't know how to use the new version to accomplish what before for them was simple? The change might eventually turn out better for them, but until they can use it, their perception will likely remain negative, perhaps into the distant future tainting any future interactions.

Something simple like including stakeholder communication from the beginning would have made their acceptance of the results much more likely. This is putting communication first.

If we keep expanding on this premise, we start to see that businesses in their most essential form are communication/information hubs that produce products and/or services instead of production organizations that use communications to make things work. Without communication nothing would get done. Let's take a moment to look at how communication is integral to every step of a manufacturing operation. Companies generate revenue by selling a product or service to a customer. Marketing communicates with prospective customers to not only learn their current needs but also what they expect to need in the future. Sales communicates with prospects to convince them to buy your products instead of those of a competitor. Engineering will design a product based on the specifications communicated to them by marketing. Manufacturing will produce the quantities of product to acceptable specifications based on the guidelines communicated to them by engineering and marketing. Manufacturing will not only communicate internally but also externally with vendors, etc. Shipping will send specific quantities of specific products to specific locations based on the guidance communicated to them from sales and operations. And so on.

Without effective communication at each of these steps, none of the organizational goals set by leadership would be possible. A communication breakdown can cause the wrong product to be developed or cause the wrong quantity to be manufactured or cause the wrong products to be shipped to the wrong address. Even the manufacturing documents are communication devices that instruct those building the products on the proper way to assemble the parts, screw in the screws and box up the product for shipping.

COMMUNICATION AS A BUSINESS PROCESS

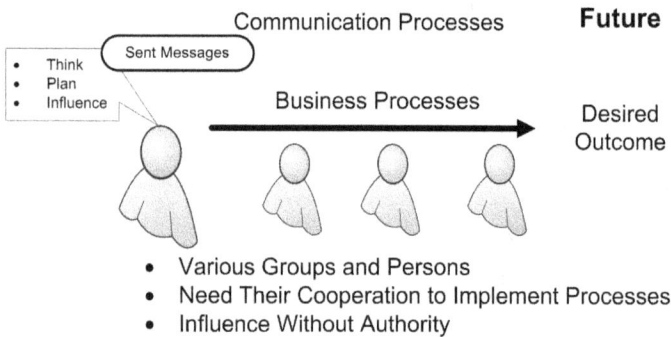

Communication Processes **Future**

Sent Messages
- Think
- Plan
- Influence

Business Processes

Desired Outcome

- Various Groups and Persons
- Need Their Cooperation to Implement Processes
- Influence Without Authority

Yet, as important as communication is to business success, it is often treated as an afterthought instead of up front as a required core competence worthy of mastery. For example, you might change a manufacturing drawing to update the specifications so that you can get that task "off your plate" but may not have considered how the changes on the drawing will affect or be interpreted by the next person in the communication chain. What if your changes are not feasible and cannot be implemented? Haven't you just undermined the very thing you are trying to accomplish? After all, your reason for making the production change is to have the person responsible for implementing the change perform the work as you intended. Shouldn't you be equally worried about getting the drawing updated as well as about making sure the changes are communicated in an understandable way to the person making the actual changes? Just sending the changes doesn't ensure that they will be understood as intended. It is integral to effective communication that the sender also ensure understanding on the part of the production person doing the work or they could incorrectly make the changes and with the best of intentions. Nobody wins in that case.

Caution ⚠

We tend to communicate from our perspective - what we think is right - with little regard for how the receiver will understand our communication. This is backwards thinking. Think about that for a moment. Considering how you plan to communicate something before you start communicating is an important first step to improved communication. Who is your audience? How do they think? How can you confirm understanding? We will discuss these and other topics throughout the rest of the book as we begin looking at communication situations from the perspective of the receiving audience.

Effective communication is a skill not a natural birthright. Yes, we can all talk from early childhood and learned how to read and write in school, but that does not make us effective communicators. To become an effective communicator, you will have to let go of some of the habits you have acquired along the way. If you knew a specific talent was critical to your success, wouldn't you take the steps needed to become as good at it as possible? Oddly enough, not with communication. It's almost as though we think this competence should happen naturally.

StreetSmarts

I am reminded of a friend who is a professional drummer for a nationally known rock band. We were sitting in a restaurant and a man at the next table started drumming with his fingers on the table. My friend looked up at me with a sarcastic look on his face and said, "Everyone's a drummer!"

It's like we think of ourselves as effective communicators even though our experience shows that this is not the case. Just as my friend stands out as an excellent drummer when others see him perform, effective communicators stand out too. Unfortunately, this means that those who think that they are "excellent communicators" look like amateurs around those who work hard to improve their communication skills. Not everyone is a drummer. Sorry.

Effective business communication takes conscious effort. It takes a willingness to see things from others' perspectives and it takes effort on your part to change old ineffective habits into those that work. The Outcome Oriented Communication™ method introduced in this book is intended for business situations where some type of organizational outcome is intended. It focuses on the use of communication as a tool to increase the likelihood of successfully achieving an outcome. Business communication is simpler than personal communication in that business communication usually occurs to create a desired (and often shared) outcome. Yes, there is interpersonal communication involved in every step of organizational communication, but the context of that communication is narrow (outcome oriented) compared to other personal situations, such as with family and friends. Knowing your desired outcome, understanding the situation, and tailoring your communication to the situation will greatly increase your odds of achieving your intended business communication outcome.

Organizational vs Personal Communication

Ineffective business communication is costly. Think about the number of meetings you have attended that were a waste of your time and likely a waste of time for the other attendees. Multiply the time spent in the meeting by the number of attendees, add the time needed for each person to prepare for and travel to/from the meeting (or commute from another city), and you get a sense of the cost of inefficient meetings. Think about the phone calls you get from people that you dread – not because they are not great people but because they waste your time. Now think about the possibility that you might be someone who wastes others' time. What if you could take steps to ensure that the time of others is respected and used to best advantage? What if you could accomplish your desired outcome with an email that recipients could read and understand in a matter of minutes instead of spending (wasting?) hours in a meeting? Doesn't it make sense that people around you would become more cooperative and responsive? This is the value of the Outcome Oriented Communication method: you will learn to think proactively about desired communication outcomes in relation to your audience before you act, greatly increasing your likelihood of achieving them.

Outcome Oriented Communication differs from typical personal communication in that it is goal focused. Efficient organizations do not typically communicate for pleasure or to pass the time. Efficient organizations communicate to move individuals, groups and eventually the entire organization in a specific, unified direction. When people communicate to focus on actions and outcomes, instead of simply "acting" like they are communicating to "get stuff done", clarity emerges and efficiency happens. Granted, there will be times when communication is not blatantly operationally oriented, such as a company-wide celebration event, but even in these situations there is a desired communication outcome. A company picnic, for example, might have a communication outcome of demonstrating that the company cares about its personnel with the hope of increasing employee satisfaction and decreasing turnover. It might also have a secondary communication outcome of providing a forum for employees from different departments to learn about each other, and to develop informal communication bridges for when unexpected operational issues later arise. You will see how important this is in the section of Chapter 5 that discusses worker experience.

When you, as the communication sender, are clear about your desired communication outcome, there is no reason to talk about topics that do not specifically pertain to the desired outcome of the moment. Should off-topic items come up, you simply schedule them for another, more pertinent time. There is little reason to involve persons who do not contribute in some way to achieving the desired outcome of a specific situation. What you think may be disrespectful in not including someone might be doing them a favor because you would not be wasting their time. Ask around and people will likely tell you that they attend too many meetings and that they would appreciate being invited only to those where their specific participation is needed. On the other hand, being invited to a meeting can have significance beyond just functionality so be sensitive to how being invited, or not invited, to a meeting will be interpreted by others. Outcome Oriented Communication is about using communication as a tool for fostering cooperation from others to help you efficiently achieve your desired functional outcomes. It is also about creating common understanding between stakeholders, which could mean inviting people to meetings where their immediate functional contribution in a particular meeting may be limited but ultimately their better understanding fosters overall greater outcome efficiency.

Business activities require the support and cooperation of others to achieve goals. If you are clear about what you want from others, and supportive of them in providing what they need to get there, you are more likely to achieve your goals. If you are not sure about what you want from others, then there isn't much mystery about why you are not getting cooperation. Others will deliver for you when you give them clarity about what you want, give them a motivation to cooperate, and support them to deliver.

The outcome-oriented methodology offers a way for you to evaluate a situation, determine your most likely desired outcomes, and then determine the best communication approach to achieve those outcomes. As you adopt this approach you will find that those with whom you communicate will appreciate the respect you show for their time and be more willing to help you achieve your goals. Nothing involving human beings is foolproof, but this approach puts the odds of success on your side.

The Incredibly Important Audience As Stakeholders

It is hard to overstate the importance of the audience to a communication. Think of the audience, or receiver, of your communication as a stakeholder. A stakeholder is someone with a vested interest in a given situation. If they are not a stakeholder of some kind, why should they care? If, on the other hand, they understand their stake in the situation they will be more motivated to make it successful.

Definition

Stakeholders are those people who have an interest in something. For example, a purchasing agent who buys parts for manufacturing would have several stakeholders: the vendor who they are negotiating with, the internal manufacturing manager who needs the parts, the engineers who prescribed the parts, quality control who verifies that the received parts meet specification, to name just a few. Whoever you are communicating with is a stakeholder, as is whoever they might represent. Naturally, you are a stakeholder as well.

The *audience* is the person(s) who receives your communication.

You are the *sender* of the communication.

In a sales situation, for example, the typical stakeholders would be the salesperson, the buying person, their respective management, and the prospective users of whatever is being purchased. There are primary and secondary stakeholders (audiences). The primary audience members are those who have a direct interest in a situation, such as the manager paying for the equipment or the corporate buyer handling the transaction. Secondary audience would be those one or more steps removed from the immediate situation yet affected by the outcome. In the same sales example, a secondary stakeholder might be the operations vice president who handled the prior purchase for equipment to be replaced by the current procurement. Or it might be the maintenance personnel who will inherit repairs of the new equipment. They might not have direct approval authority over the purchase, but they have an interest and exert influence in the decision.

PRIMARY AND SECONDARY AUDIENCES

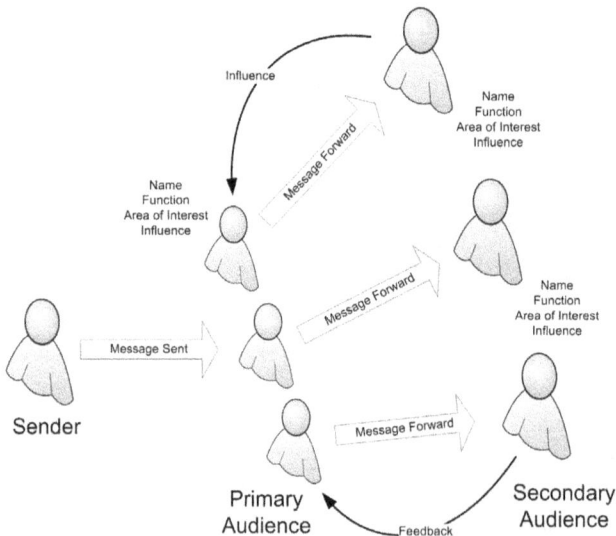

Stepping back from a communication situation to consider the primary and secondary audiences is useful, especially when a situation has potential strategic impact beyond the immediate transaction such as with a national account sales situation. In today's globally connected world, it is reasonable to expect that whatever is communicated to one person might be disclosed to another and in a short period of time. It is becoming common practice for online meetings to be recorded and then shared openly or emailed to others. Considering the reactions and desired outcomes from secondary stakeholders when communicating can save a lot of explaining down the road when they find out something you had not considered.

Making a stakeholder map will help you keep track of the various players and their interests. Start with the immediate communication situation in the center and then draw a circle for the primary stakeholders, listing their names, functions, and key areas of interest. Then draw a second level of circles for secondary stakeholders, including their names, functions, key areas of interest and potential influence on the situation. This may sound like it would only apply to sales situations, but mapping gives clarity to any situation where you need to motivate those with influence on your desired outcome. That which appears true on the surface of a communication with the primary audience may be a small part of what is happening in the background with the secondary stakeholders. Given that so many of us have jobs with much responsibility and little direct authority, learning effective ways of influencing decisions involving secondary audiences is a useful talent to cultivate.

StreetSmarts

As you communicate with others, whether speaking or in writing, you should always keep a monitor running in the back of your mind that is asking, "How would you feel if this was published as a headline in tomorrow's daily paper?" More than one leader has regretted making an off the cuff comment thinking nobody was listening only to spend the next few days explaining or defending something that they should not have said in the first place. If it doesn't need to be said, then maybe is should remain that way.

The key takeaway from this process is that it is recommended to "guestimate" how communication will happen in the future between the various stakeholders as they evaluate the situation. Which stakeholder wants a specific outcome? How do the various stakeholder outcomes align with, or conflict with, each other? How can you facilitate information and/or message transfer between stakeholders to create alignment toward meeting your goals? This is all a proactive process that if implemented conscientiously greatly increases the likelihood of your achieving your outcome.

Influencing Without Authority

It is common for someone to be responsible for a given outcome and yet have no authority over those who will help achieve that outcome. Being the responsible person for a specific business outcome means that you are the person everyone will look to for guidance and focus or (blame?) if the outcome is not successful. Typical roles like this would be national account manager or project manager roles.

Let's take a closer look at the role of the national account manager. This person acts as a communication conduit between the customer and her employer. There may be hundreds of people involved in various areas of support for her national account but few (if any) of them report directly to our account manager. These people will work in engineering, manufacturing, marketing, shipping or other departments that are most likely supporting other major accounts and managers as well. Our account manager does not have authority over these people or departments but she does have responsibility for making sure that her particular customer remains satisfied which is dependent on the service provided by these supporting department personnel. She has responsibility for her account's satisfaction but has no direct authority over those who will substantially determine that customer's level of satisfaction: this is responsibility without authority.

Definition

Responsibility without authority means that a person is responsible for delivering a certain result but does not have control over those who will make that result happen. The responsible person does not have direct report control over these key people and must influence them to act such that the desired outcome is achieved. It's a tricky job and one that requires great communication as well as organizational awareness to successfully accomplish.

The communication *message* is the thing that you want the receiver of your communication to clearly understand and remember. The message is a concept that forms in the mind of the receiver from the various communication actions you take such as a phone call, email, etc. If someone asks the receiver, "What was that email about?" the message is the thing you want them to say.

Outcome Oriented Communication helps our manager to determine the best method of communication among involved personnel. The account manager must be capable of reading and tapping into not only the needs of her primary communication audience but also the secondary (influencing) audiences as well. Situation analysis and stakeholder influence determination are key to determining not only the most effective method of communication but, very importantly, the messages to be delivered. We will define the message as the primary thing you want someone to remember from your communication. The way in which that message is delivered is covered in detail in later chapters. The primary audience for a given communication may have a set of specific, very personal, reasons for cooperating (or not cooperating) but the secondary audience (such as upper management) may have (likely will have) a very different, less personal view. For example, the department manager might not personally like our account manager, but her upper management may instead only care about keeping the customer happy. Should the department manager become difficult, our account manager could use pressure from upper management to gain cooperation. Carefully considering interaction with the primary audience (the department manager) while simultaneously keeping the secondary audience (upper management) informed might engage authority in ways not obvious from the primary communication. This can all come from strategically crafting your communications to address interests of multiple audiences.

Beware, however, that involving secondary audiences can be a double-edged sword - if their involvement is not efficiently and effectively used, it can be disastrous for the account manager. For example, inviting upper management to a time-consuming meeting when the outcomes could have been accomplished with a simple email may make it harder to receive their later support. On the other hand, not involving them personally and losing the account when upper management believes that they could have saved the account in a personal meeting can also spell disaster for our account manager. Knowing when, at what level and how to involve upper management is complicated and the Outcome Oriented Communication approach provides our account manage with a way for making this evaluation.

The project manager is another person who must apply influence without authority. A project is an activity that is outside of the normal daily operation of the business and will typically have a specified duration, budget and intended result. Larger projects may require the support of many departments and by their nature will involve group interaction. It is the project manager's responsibility to ensure that all the various groups and people are moving in a coordinated way toward the desired outcome. Effective communication is at the heart of any well-run project.

The project manager's goal is to complete a project within a specified timeframe, within budget and to the intended specifications. It is surprising the number of projects that are delivered late (or cancelled), materially over budget and/or delivered but not meeting intended specifications. Project management professionals agree that effective communication is critically important to project success. They will tell you that a difficult part of their job is being held responsible for delivering outcomes while having little authority over those who will perform the work. Quite often project managers are required to work not only across departments within their own company but also between different companies as well. The successful project manager must become proficient at motivating a potentially large, geographically dispersed, diverse group of workers over whom they have no authority to move toward a common goal. The perception of whether a project was successful or not is dependent up on how progress is communicated to stakeholders. Sometimes successful projects can go unnoticed and communicating the success is important for team morale and career recognition. Should a project not be meeting its goals, effective communication along the way can help to keep from damaging client relationships. Treating communication as an afterthought in a project management environment is like a housing general contractor not reading the blueprints before starting to build.

Groups and Communication

Businesses have employees because many people should be able to accomplish more than a single individual. Today's organizations involve people from various functional areas and cultures who will each have a direct impact on the likelihood of successfully achieving company goals. Most of us have experienced situations where throwing more people at a problem didn't solve the problem more quickly, or at all. Instead of things more rapidly steaming to a successful conclusion through team alignment, chaos resulted as these groups of new people started to pull in their own direction instead of as a team. Creating alignment requires communication. Determining group goals involves communication. Coordinating individuals toward achieving those goals involves communication. Acknowledging successful completion of goals involves communication. Communication is the glue that binds together successful groups.

Chapter Summary

Hopefully you can now see how considering communication as an afterthought makes little sense in today's communication intensive world. Whenever more than one person is involved, communication is needed. We may communicate differently based on personality or cultural differences, but we communicate as a natural part of who we are. Business communication focuses our communication toward accomplishing agreed upon goals. Others will make judgments about you based in large part on the quality and effectiveness of your ability to communicate. High quality people with much to offer can undermine their work effectiveness and careers by not being perceived as effective communicators. People who are technically less qualified can successfully progress within an organization due to their excellent perceived ability to communicate.

Becoming a great communicator makes practical sense. Arguably the most efficient way to have others support your goals is to communicate in a way that motivates them to support your desired outcomes. Using the Outcome Oriented Communication method will help you determine the most desirable and likely outcomes for a given situation, create a message that motivates others to support your outcomes, and determine the best communication approach for delivering your message.

Communication Is More Than Sending A Message

Many incorrectly believe that after they have mailed a letter, sent an email, or held a meeting, that communication has happened. Think about the number of times you have been asked by someone what so-in-so's email meant or what they interpreted from a meeting, only to find out that their takeaway from the communication was completely different from yours. The same message was interpreted differently by two different people, which is likely not what the sender intended. Taking a communication-related action does not in itself comprise communication, and it certainly does not mean that the outcome you wanted from the communication will happen. Effective communication involves a symbiosis between the sender of a message and the intended audience. If you don't start communicating by first considering the audience, you are already on a losing track. Remember that communication happens in the mind of your audience – if they didn't understand what you communicated to them in the way you intended, then effective communication did not happen. This chapter offers complete communication concepts and their application, providing an important foundation for understanding the overall Outcome Oriented Communication method.

The Complete Communication Model

Here is an idea that should be obvious but will be a revelation to most people: communication is not complete until the receiver of your message has received and understood your message as you intended. This means that communication involves *both* the sender and the receiver, with a heavier emphasis on the receiver. This is a critical concept that I hope you will take a moment to process. Your intent for communicating is to create some type of understanding in the mind of your message receiver, or you would not be communicating in the first place. Not considering the receiver (audience) characteristics makes no sense in this context, and we will look deeply at the audience in Chapter 5. Effective communication does not mean that the receiver will agree with the sender or will do what the sender requests. Creating agreement is accomplished by the contents of the message sent. Complete communication only means that the receiver has understood your message as you initially intended.

Take a moment to reflect on the number of problems you have encountered in your life that were caused by miscommunication – one person intended to say one thing only to have the other interpret it in another way. Minimizing miscommunication allows workers to focus on creating desired business outcomes instead of arguing about phantom problems caused by an avoidable misunderstanding.

Here is something else that makes little sense and yet is common: Senders often treat communication like it is the receiver's job to properly understand the message, and if their understanding does not match that intended by the sender, it is the receiver's "fault." The problem with this approach is that being "right" as the sender about how effectively we communicated does not help us if the receiver does not do what we asked based on miscommunication. This is particularly unfortunate when the receiver would have cooperated if he had only understood the message in the way it was initially intended by the sender.

THE COMPLETE COMMUNICATION MODEL

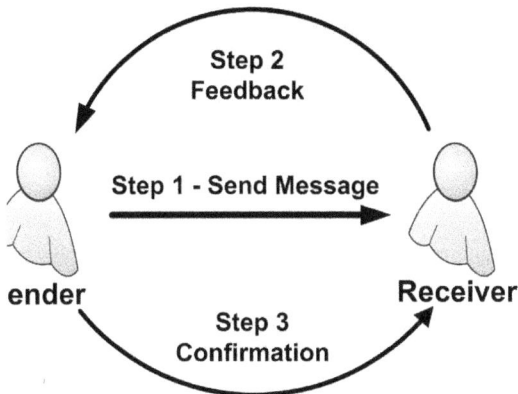

Complete communication removes ambiguity between what you (the *sender*) intend from a message and what is understood by your audience (the *receiver*). There are three basic steps to the complete communication model: 1) You send the message to the audience (receiver), 2) Your audience receives the message and then repeats his interpretation of the message back to you (*feedback*), and 3) You confirm to your receiver that his interpretation was correct or explain where it did not match your intent (*Confirmation*). Steps 2 and 3 may need to be repeated until the sender and receiver have an agreement on the message content. Notice that after this process is fully completed, you have verification that your receiver understood your message in exactly the way you intended. This is complete communication. As mentioned earlier, this does not mean that you, as the sender, will get cooperation, but at least you have been understood as intended.

StreetSmarts

I had a boss who was slow in responding to my emails, which frustrated me. When I pushed him on his slowness, he said something I never forgot. "I get hundreds of emails a day, and all are important. Why should I read yours over the others? Plus, it takes me a long time to read through your emails to get to the essence of what you are trying to say. If you want me to read them, make them worth reading." This was one of my early encounters with the cost of not considering my audience when communicating.

Most people think of communication as step one: sending the message. After that, it is up to the receiver to figure it out. Notice that stopping at step one does not confirm that the message was understood as intended or even received at all. If your goal in communicating was to have your message understood by another person, you should see that if you stop at Step 1 and your message is incorrectly understood or not received at all, your communication purpose (*outcome*) will not happen. Even worse, your message might be incorrectly interpreted in such a way that it causes more problems in the mind of the receiver than existed in the first place. Instead of your step-one communication helping to solve problems, your ineffective communication can create problems that were not there at the beginning.

Steps two and three of the Complete Communication Model verify for both you and your receiver that your message was interpreted as intended. If the receiver misunderstands, steps 2 and 3 allow discourse between you and them to clear up the misunderstanding. In this way, the sender can revise and resend the message with the goal of improving understanding. Without steps two and three, you are sending a message in a vacuum and have no way of knowing if the message was received as intended or not. Essentially, you are broadcasting a message and hoping that it is properly understood.

This is how most people communicate – sending first and then thinking (or worrying) about understanding afterward. This approach may make you feel more productive, but it doesn't achieve understanding in any consistent way and can cause problems that weren't there in the first place.

Caution ⚠

Have you ever sent an important text message or email to someone and not heard back from them in a timely manner? Think about what went through your head as you waited for their reply. Were they angry? Disappointed? Busy? OK? Apathetic? It's possible that your later texts escalated with intensity in response to their not responding. I've even seen people rebuke someone for not responding. In my case, the receiver of my texts needed to replace her phone, and she never got my messages. All the stuff going through my head had nothing to do with reality. She hadn't even received the messages and, indeed, was wondering why she hadn't heard from me. My earlier communications were locked in step 1 of the model. Completing Steps 2 and three would have handled all of that in an instant. It's strange how reality is almost always more benign than what we can make up left to our own mental devices.

The Complete Communication Model is a simple process that would ideally be done between two people in a noise-proof room with perfect lighting and all other ideal environmental conditions. Real communication situations are much more complex and challenging.

Senders approach communication with their own set of beliefs about communication in general and this communication in particular. Receivers approach communication with their own belief set, which will differ from those of the sender. The external environment and specific tools used affect communication, as does the inherent difficulty of communicating something in a way that is without alternate interpretation. Any number of factors can compromise communication, and the more important your need for communication clarity, the more imperative it is that you consider these factors *before* communicating.

A MORE COMPLICATED AND REALISTIC COMMUNICATION ENVIRONMENT

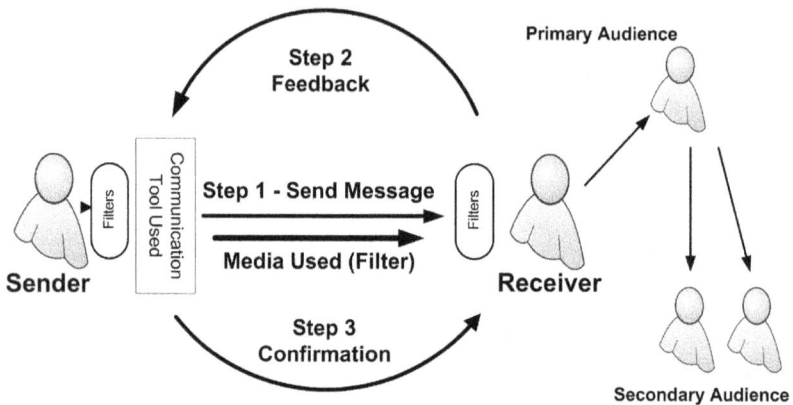

The Roles of Communication Hygiene Factors and Filters

It is challenging to communicate clearly when "clearly" is defined as communicating in a way that is not open to alternate interpretations. Two people talking alone in a room with no distractions will often have difficulty communicating without misunderstanding. In realistic and less ideal circumstances, personal as well as environmental factors further impede clear communication. These factors are referred to as communication "barriers" in that they are potential stumbling blocks to clear communication. Typical barriers would include cultural differences (such as language), education and experience differences, physical factors such as noisy or broken connections, mental distractions, and/or interpersonal issues between the sender and receiver.

As an example, let's start with something as common as a telephone call between two managers – one from the United States and the other from Japan. We first have the issues associated with simply making the telephone call, such as the phone number itself, international dialing instructions, getting past assistants who do not speak English, time zone differences, and the like. Think of these as the communication equivalent of "hygiene factors," as defined by Frederick Herzberg in his book "The Motivation to Work," which is related to employee management and motivation theory.[1] Herzberg refers to hygiene factors as those factors that must be in place for an employee to "show up" for the job and include adequate salary, a safe working environment, adequate transportation, a place to work, and other similar items. According to Herzberg, offering proper hygiene factors does not ensure that the employee will be motivated to performance excellence. The factors only provide the necessary basics for excellence to show up. Not providing them creates major stumbling blocks in creating excellent performance.

What we will call *communication hygiene factors* are those factors that must be present for complete communication to occur. If you have ever been invited to a meeting at a specific time but not been told where the meeting was being held, you have experienced the lack of a communication hygiene factor. Herzberg does not claim that including a hygiene factor ensures that an employee will be satisfied with the work environment, only that not including a hygiene factor will create dissatisfaction. This is analogous to communication in that including the location of a meeting does not ensure that the meeting will have a satisfactory result. Not including the location does, however, ensure that the intended meeting outcomes will not be achieved. Nobody will be there but you.

> ## Caution ⚠
>
> I worked with a manager who liked to call meetings at the last minute and then not provide us all with the needed hygiene factors for the meeting to occur. For example, for a face-to-face meeting, she would send out the time but not the location. For a teleconference, she would include the conference number but not the PIN needed for our specific meeting. She once called for a GoToMeeting (which she rarely used) without even checking if people knew what GoToMeeting was. Everyone scrambled to install the software, learn how to use it, and upgrade their software in preparation for the meeting, only to have her cancel the meeting 15 minutes after it was scheduled to start (after not showing up). Needless to say, in the future, we all gave a collective groan every time we received a meeting invitation from her. Hers was not an effective way to achieve support from others to achieve her organizational outcomes.

Logistical (hygiene) factors must be dealt with to create the possibility of communication, and careful consideration in advance of any communication is necessary. Unfortunately, they are often overlooked as senders focus their attention on the various aspects of the communication message itself and not on the foundation elements that are needed for clear communication to occur.

Typical Communication Hygiene Factors

Letter	Email	Individual Phone	Teleconfer- ence/Video Conference	Individual Meeting	Group Meeting
Language	Language	Language	Language	Language	Language
Time (zone)	Time (zone)	Time (zone)	Time (zone)	Time (zone)	Time (zone)
Physical address	Email ad- dresses	Phone num- ber	Conference number/PIN	Physical location	Physical location adequate for group needs
Return physical address	Return email address (personal/ private)	Connection clarity (cell phone)	Proper software installed	Travel schedules	Travel schedules
	Spam filters		Technology	Physical security access	Physical security access
		Time coor- dination	Group coor- dination	Time coor- dination	Group time and location co- ordination
De Facto	De Facto	De Facto	Technology consider- ations	Technology consider- ations	Technology consider- ations

Note: De Facto indicates that these communication media are fairly standard, and the likelihood of this factor becoming a barrier is minimal. In other words, most people know how to read a letter, talk on the phone or send an email with minimal training.

Let's return to the phone call example. Assume that both parties are on the telephone at the same time and that the basic connection-related hygiene factors are in place. The two communicators can hear each other speak.

They now must address the language hygiene factor. If no common language exists between them, then no communication can occur. Interpreters must be available during the conversation adding another level of human filter and logistical complexity.

Our two communicators can now hear and understand each other through the interpreters. So far, so good. Now it is time for the cultural filters to show up. Assume that the American jumps right into the business aspect of the conversation with minimal of what he calls "superfluous" discussion only to get frustrated with the Japanese party's repeatedly shifting the conversation from business to more general matters. Notice that our two communicators can hear each other talking on the phone, they understand each other's words through interpreters, and yet this phone call will most likely lead to frustrating and unproductive results for both parties due to cultural barriers. It is a common business practice in Japan to place heavier emphasis on developing a relationship before getting into the specifics of any business negotiation. Our American may think that he is being respectful of the other party's time by getting straight to the point when he is actually undermining his likelihood of success by not appreciating this important Japanese cultural norm.

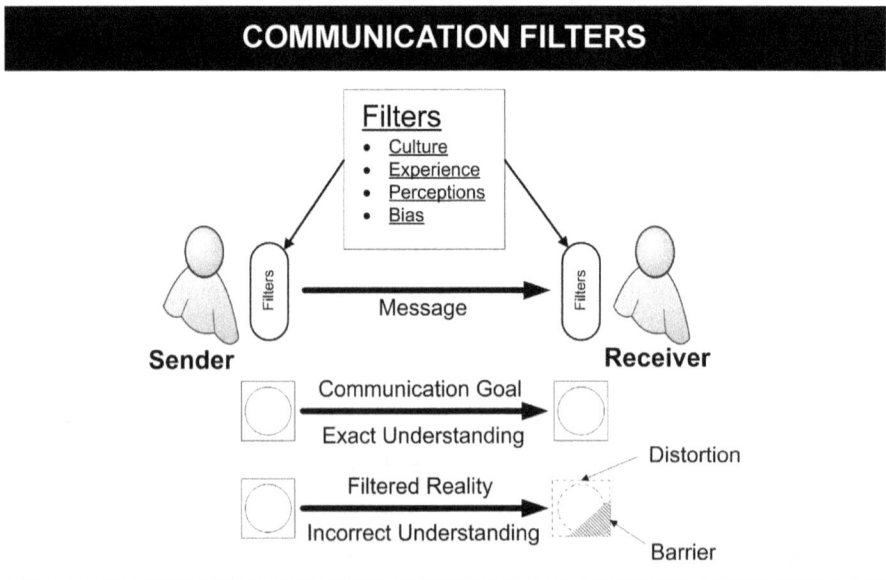

COMMUNICATION FILTERS

The perception barriers presented in the prior example are called *filters,* and they permeate all levels of communication. Filters affect how things are interpreted by both sender and receiver. For example, if the sender has the belief that all business should be transacted in English, then he is unlikely to attempt communication in another language.

StreetSmarts

It is a common error for those new to business to focus on the tangible, rational, justifiable aspects of business and not pay adequate attention to the human filters that underlie all communication. As a new salesperson, I made this mistake, and it cost me. I had just been promoted to Regional Sales Manager for a five-state central region of the USA. Fresh out of college and sales training school, I contacted the existing customers in the region and got nowhere. They were glacially polite when meeting with me, at best, and the conversations were short and tense. I was finally brave enough to ask a customer why he was so cold with me, and he explained that my predecessor had said a lot of the same things I was saying and then abandoned him after closing the deal. He had bought a lot of expensive equipment that never functioned as he was led by the salesperson to believe, and it stagnated his career. The equipment was sitting on the production floor, covered by dusty tarps. To this day, the memory makes me sad. Any wonder he didn't trust me? His filter was saying "liar, liar" to everything I said, whether he realized it or not. By the way, I corrected the neglect of my predecessor, got his equipment running, and personally trained him and other engineers at the company on how to use it correctly. His career got back on track, and so did my quota.

The American is getting everything he wants from the conversation – he is speaking English, he is talking to a decision maker and getting right to the point, making what he believes is an effective use of both parties' time. His filters are fully satisfied. The problem is that he is not considering the perception filters in place on the Japanese side of the conversation, which are challenged by having to speak English and by the lack of pleasantries that he believes are needed before moving into a business discussion. This is the type of scenario in which the American gets off the phone thinking things went great, and the Japanese party ends the call knowing he will never do business with him. Not considering filters before starting an important communication is a mistake. Before communicating, always step back for a moment to think about how the world looks in the mind of your intended receiver. Again, there is a lot of information related to understanding your audience in Chapter 5, and here are a few things you can try to better understand your audience's filters.

Have you had dealings with this person (audience) before? Were they favorable or a disaster? How experienced is your audience with you, your company, and your topic? Is their perception of you and your company positive, negative, or neutral? Is there any kind of personal connection between your audience and you or other stakeholders that could influence their listening filters? If you were your audience, why would they be interested in your intended communication (or not)? What would get them interested and willing to cooperate?

Finally, you could consider something as simple as asking your audience how they would like you to communicate with them. I have found that people appreciate it when I ask them things such as how to pronounce their name, if it has a unique spelling, or when and how are the best ways to communicate with them. If nothing else, they appreciate the courtesy, as I would as well.

StreetSmarts

One of my favorite and most powerful advance planning questions is this: What must happen during the communication to cause the audience to think that the time they invested in understanding the communication was well spent? I find holding this question in my mind while preparing the communication provides a powerful context that keeps me focused. It forces me to think like them, which is hugely important.

Much has been written about communication filters, and a detailed discussion of filters is beyond the scope of this book.[2] What is important to understand is that a filter is anything that can interfere with creating complete understanding between you and your message audience. So far, we have talked about the filters that exist in the minds of the involved persons. It turns out the media that you use for your communication injects its own filter that few people know about or even consider. The following section will briefly introduce media richness theory which is so important that Chapter 3 is dedicated to it.

Let's look at a simple example of how a simple perception filter can create misunderstanding and problems when both sender and receiver are cooperatively working towards the same intended outcome.

Think about something as simple as the color blue. When you read "blue," a color likely popped into your head, and you knew exactly what I was talking about. Here is the problem – I was looking at a blue-colored item sitting on my desk that is almost certainly not the same color that you visualized. If we both continue forward as though we are thinking about the exact same shade of blue without confirming the shade, then the likelihood of a mismatch being found later on is high. If the shade of blue is important to the outcome of our communication, then getting agreement about which shade of blue we are discussing would be warranted. A mismatch in the perception of the color blue would be a communication filter (barrier) because it interferes with complete understanding.

Pantone, Inc. recognized this problem in the early 1960s when working within the printing industry.[3] An artwork designer would use a specific group of colors for their design, and people printing the work had difficulty getting a precise color match. Much frustration and expense were wasted trying to match the final printed product colors to those intended by the original artist. Pantone developed a color matching system so that a designer could select a color from the Pantone palette and specify that color as part of the design. The printer would know that by using the same specified Pantone color, they would print the work so that the colors exactly matched those intended by the designer. The Pantone color matching system was created to facilitate effective communication, and it is still in wide use today. Here is an example of an entire standard created to simply facilitate complete communication between designers and printers.

As your awareness of communication barriers and filters becomes more acute, you will often see opportunities for improvement. It could be something as simple as a door sign that indicates a room needs cleaning. The goal of the room owner is to work in a clean room, and the cleaning crew is happy to clean the room if they know it needs cleaning. The barrier, in this case, is timing. The staff is likely at home sleeping when the cleaning crew is working. The link across the barrier is a simple door sign indicating that the room needs cleaning that will be understood as such by the audience, the cleaning crew. Thinking in advance about potential barriers to this simple communication, if they only speak Polish, then it would make sense to create the sign in both English and Polish, don't you think? Problem solved with a little communication forethought.

Communication Media Richness Overview

The Paulson Media Matching Method, presented in detail in Chapter Six, considers the communication connection (*link*) itself as part of the communication, almost like a hygiene factor. All delivery media, such as email, text messaging, telephone, or face-to-face meetings, are not equally suited for message delivery. Just as ensuring proper message delivery is important to not creating later problems, selecting the proper communication media is necessary to ensure that a media mismatch does not in itself create problems. The framework for understanding media differences presented here is derived from media richness theory as initially presented in 1984 by Daft and Lengel.[4] The details are covered in "Chapter Three: Media Richness and Feedback Concepts." According to media richness theory, different media are categorized on a scale from lean to rich based on the ability to communicate information and different communication situations are best suited for specific media types.

StreetSmarts

Here it is important to separate the method of communication (media) from the message being communicated. A poorly crafted message well delivered using the approach presented in this book will likely not get you your desired outcome because your audience will not like what they understood. Conversely, a well-crafted message delivered poorly using either the incorrect media or with poor skills will not be properly understood and, again, not get you your desired outcome. The importance of the message itself cannot be overstated. For this reason, crafting the message is the focus of the entire Second Book in this book series, "Getting Agreement." Combining great message creation with proper media selection puts the odds of communication success on your side.

Leaner broadcast-type media, such as print magazines, provide little opportunity for feedback from the receiver to sender creating a situation where the sender may never know whether the sent message was received as intended. More rich media, such as face-to-face meetings, allow the sender to monitor the receiver's reactions on a real-time basis offering feedback about the level of message understanding. If the receiver's understanding is incorrect, the sender can see that and quickly adjust the message and resend it, which is not possible using very lean media. Even more troubling is that selecting the improper media for a message can create misunderstandings and problems that were not there in the first place. The combination of the Outcome Oriented Communication method and the Paulson Media Matching Method offers a process whereby senders can develop not only the right message for the right situation but also select the media most likely to clearly and completely communicate the message to ensure proper understanding. Book Two in this series is dedicated to message development.

The Important and Ignored Message – Receiver - Media Selection Relationship

Remember that the receiver of your communication decides whether he will help you get your desired outcome, so there is an intrinsic communication relationship between sender and receiver. As the sender, you are not powerless in this situation in that you are creating the framework for your intended communication. That power is applied in communicating with the receiver in a way that makes the most sense to him.

Different people will communicate in different ways. Some may prefer rich communication media (always meeting face-to-face), whereas others would prefer never to talk directly to another human being ("email me, and I will email back my thoughts"). We have all known people who draw their energy from others and need the stimulation derived from a face-to-face encounter. Yet there are others who view dealing with people as an intrusion, and they would happily always communicate by email or not at all. It turns out that different media are best suited for different situations, which means that our natural communication styles may be best suited for certain situations and potentially harmful to others. Understanding your natural communication style is an important place to start so that you can rein in your natural tendencies in favor of the communication style that is most likely to achieve your intended outcome.

THE OUTCOME-ORIENTED COMMUNICATION MODEL

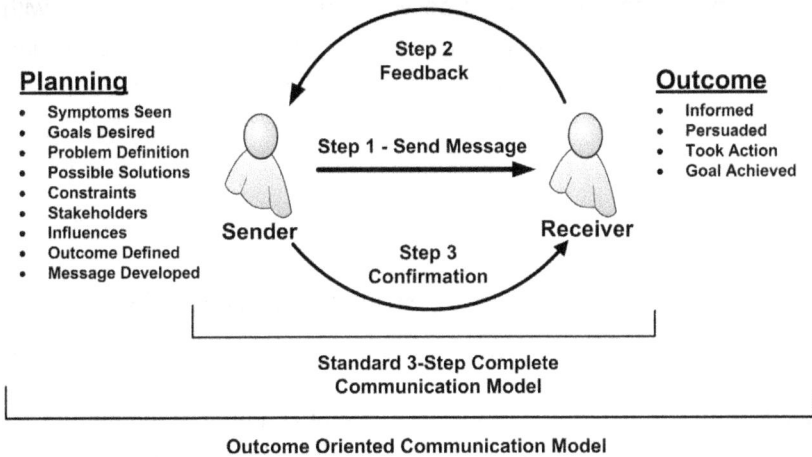

Planning
- Symptoms Seen
- Goals Desired
- Problem Definition
- Possible Solutions
- Constraints
- Stakeholders
- Influences
- Outcome Defined
- Message Developed

Step 2
Feedback

Step 1 - Send Message

Sender

Step 3
Confirmation

Receiver

Outcome
- Informed
- Persuaded
- Took Action
- Goal Achieved

Standard 3-Step Complete
Communication Model

Outcome Oriented Communication Model

It is also important to consider the de-facto learning style of your intend-ed audience. All groups will not learn or interact with you in similar ways. Expert groups will not want to wade through a lot of background information to get at the essence of a presentation or report. Experts will typically re-spond best to a direct presentation of the salient facts and rely on your critical analysis of the topic. Less experienced groups will usually get lost in a direct presentation that does not provide a much larger contextual understanding. As a result, a presentation to a less experienced group will be better received if a "softer" approach is used. Adjusting the communication approach to the audience characteristics puts your likelihood of communication outcome success on the positive side.

StreetSmarts

It is becoming common to develop live presentations or written correspondences with the Bottom Line On Top (BLOT) approach, which presents the major audience takeaway succinctly at the beginning. The assumption is that if your audience does not have much time, they will get the gist of what you are communicating quickly. They can decide for themselves if they want to hear or read more at that point. This is similar to the "inverted pyramid" approach used in the newspaper business, where the essence of a story is delivered in the first 1-3 sentences with supporting details included deeper into the article. The concept is that busy commuters may not have time to read the entire article, but they can quickly scan the title and first few sentences to remain informed. More about message flow is included in Book 2: "Getting Agreement."

Confirming Received Understanding Using Feedback

As mentioned earlier, confirming proper receipt and understanding of a sent message is intrinsic to complete communication. The method of confirmation will change based on the feedback capabilities of the communication media used and environmental circumstances, which means that building some type of confirmation process into a communication plan is very important. Without feedback of some kind, the sender never really knows if the receiver got the message at all, let alone understood it as intended. At this stage of the book, simply adopt the belief that message comprehension feedback is very important and think about how you, as the sender, will determine proper receipt and understanding before sending your messages. We'll get into feedback in more detail in Chapter Three. By the way, it is important for receivers to confirm proper receipt as well. If you are the receiver of an important message, you can help promote complete communication by asking the sender for confirmation of your understanding to ensure both parties are on the same page. A simple yet critical takeaway from this quick section is this – you should always build ways for getting feedback into your communication plans.

Chapter Summary

Most people believe that they have communicated when they send an email, leave a text, leave a voice mail, or send a snail mail letter. This is a self-centered instead of an audience-centered approach and can cause future problems as audiences interpret messages in their own ways instead of those intended by the sender. All humans have perception filters that shade our understanding of what is communicated to us. Without a thorough understanding of the audience, it is impossible to accurately predict how your audience will interpret your message. We will see in the next chapter that the media selected for sending the message injects its own filter into the messaging process as well.

Complete communication only happens when a message sent by one person is understood by the receiver (audience) exactly as intended by the sender. The Outcome Oriented Communication approach encourages the sender to proactively evaluate a business situation and then to develop a message and communication approach specific to their intended audience and situation. This chapter presented fundamental communication concepts that are a foundation upon which we will build the Outcome Oriented Communication and Paulson Media Matching Method. Always remember to consider the audience, your desired outcome, and feedback possibilities before communicating, and you will find people more cooperative in helping you achieve your business goals.

Media Richness And Feedback Concepts

Y ou can see from the prior chapter that communication barriers are a major impediment to complete communication. Unfortunately, these barriers are real and must be dealt with if there is any chance of achieving the complete message understanding we seek. The most reliable way to deal with them is to facilitate some type of feedback mechanism into our communication that allows us to determine if our message was received as intended. This would be Steps 2 and 3 of the Complete Communication Model presented in Chapter 2. You can think of this feedback as a type of quality control check. Even under the best communication circumstances confirming complete communication is challenging. Here is the problem in today's business world: we are rarely in the same room with each other, which makes it even more difficult to complete these two important steps. Daily we may use email, text messaging, group video conferencing, chat, instant messaging, etc., instead of talking in person or face-to-face. On the other hand, without these two steps that offer feedback and message confirmation, we are leaving ourselves open to miscommunication which creates its own problems. Facilitating steps 2 and 3 in today's communication technology-rich environment is a combination of technology, science, and personal style, all functioning based on media richness theory concepts.

I was first introduced to *media richness theory* in the late 1980s, just a few years after the concepts were introduced by Daft and Lengel.[1] Their basic concept was that the different media (e.g., written report, email, text, video, face-to-face, etc.) have different communication capabilities and, as such, should not be treated as interchangeable but instead should be uniquely matched for specific communication needs. The approach made immediate sense to me, having spent the prior decade working in various Silicon Valley sales, engineering, and project management roles, most of which were heavily electronic communication dependent because stakeholders were geographically dispersed. I liked that the theory offered a structured approach to determining the best communication approach to use for a given communication situation. I had learned the hard way that different situations required different communication approaches but had not formalized my thinking in this area.

At that time, communication mediums were limited compared to those available today, making the theory even more relevant today. I have since adapted and expanded upon the theory in my academic and professional work. This chapter represents a blend of initial concepts, additional concepts developed by others, and best practices I have adopted in my over 20 years of experience experimenting with communication media selection. To understand the influence of media selection, we must first understand the components of the message delivery system from sender to receiver. Always remember that a primary goal of communication is to create complete understanding between sender and receiver.

Relating the Message, Transmission Channel, the Media and Richness

The intent of communication is to send a message which contains content that communicates a specific meaning from the sender to the receiving audience. The goal of the communication process is to deliver this message.

Something must link the sender to the receiver of the message, or it will not be delivered. There is some type of connection technology that carries the information, such as coaxial cable, fiber optic cable, telephone wire, cellular, printed paper, Wi-Fi, Bluetooth, etc., which we will call the communication *channel*. The media is a service (or tool) that operates using channels such as video conferences, television, radio, newspaper, text messaging, telephone, etc. The *richness* of media is directly related to the timeliness of audience feedback plus the information level offered between the audience and the sender. This is a lot to take in all at once, and a couple of examples will help with understanding it all.

Definition

The *message* is the conceptual idea that you intend to convey to the receiver of your communication. The *media* is the communication tool used to convey the message, such as e-mail, text, or video conference. The *channel* is the underlying technology used by the media to deliver the message. *Feedback* is a way for the sender of a message to determine if the receiver understood the message as intended. *Broadcast* media are those that have little to no feedback, such as television, radio, or newspaper.

Let's look at broadcast television to explain this differentiation. In its original form, television was a broadcast media meaning that the television folks developed content (the message) based on their best guess of what television watchers wanted to see, and they then transmitted it through the air (the channel) to the living room television set. Producers had no way of knowing if people watched or liked the programs because there was no way for viewers to offer feedback. Due to this lack of feedback, broadcast media would be considered to have lower media richness.

Companies like Nielsen (www.nielsen.com) saw this feedback void and developed a tracking system that provided the producers with a measurement (rating) of how many viewers were watching their shows. Armed with this new knowledge, the show producers could develop more shows like those people watched the most and cancel those that had low popularity. Think of the show content as the message, television broadcast as the sending media (step 1), and Nielsen as the feedback (step 2). Based on the feedback, the producers produced similar content (step 3), and an increase in Nielsen rating told the producers that the viewers approved, and so forth. Notice that without the feedback, the producers would always be guessing about which show to produce next. Notice also that there was a major time delay between when the initial show was broadcast and when the revised show, based on viewer feedback, could be shown. This second scenario includes feedback which means it is a richer media than a simple broadcast, but it is still a low-richness approach compared to other options.

Let's see what a similar television show looks like in today's connected world. That same show may still be broadcast over the air to a living room antenna, but it may also be streamed through your cable provider or offered online through a website. The over-the-air broadcast has similar feedback limitations as before and has low media richness but look at what happens to richness levels with the other two options. Through the cable providers, the producers get viewer feedback immediately in that they quickly know how many households viewed the show and who they are. The faster feedback and additional information increase the richness level compared to the previous broadcast approach. Through the website delivery method, the producers can get even more detailed and immediate feedback from viewers on what they liked or disliked by incorporating surveys that interact with viewers during the show making the richness of this scenario even higher. In those instances where the viewers can choose their own version of how the show will proceed based on interactions during the show, the producers get immediate receiver feedback which causes the show to immediately adapt, which further increases the richness level.

We can apply a similar analysis to your local newspaper, which may arrive at your house through different channels such as print or over the Internet. The print version is low richness, like the broadcast television example from before, in that the publishers write and print stories that they believe their readers want to read and use the subscription numbers as a surrogate for approval (sort of like Nielsen). But when the stories are read online, the publishers get immediate feedback about which stories are most popular, which ones were read in more detail, and which reporters are most followed, which makes the interactive nature of online newspapers far richer than the print version. The feedback is immediate and contains more useful information, which increases the richness.

To summarize, when we talk about media richness, we are talking about a blend of feedback availability, the timeliness of the feedback, and the level of information contained within the feedback. We are not talking about the speed of the transmission method, such as fiber optic or telephone wiring. We can send the same broadcast newspaper over a high-speed fiber optic line, and it will still have the same low richness level unless feedback and receiver information is provided.

You may be wondering, at this point, why should you care about all of this? It turns out that all media are not created equal, and certain communication media are better suited to certain communication situations. In addition, a specific message for a specific audience may ideally require a higher level of media richness than you are able to use. In this case, understanding the shortcomings imposed by the leaner media allows you to consider other approaches to compensate for what is lost from using the leaner richness. Selecting the proper communication media will greatly improve the likelihood of your message being understood as intended. We will see later that selecting the wrong media for a given situation can create problems that were not there in the first place, an undesirable outcome by any measure. The Media richness level is important and little understood. The more you understand and apply it, the more successful you will be as a communicator.

Recall from an earlier chapter that complete communication does not mean that the receiver is going to agree with you. The message must be designed to foster the desired cooperation or agreement. Media richness consideration is required to best ensure that your message is understood as you intended: to foster complete communication. There is no guarantee that after somebody understands your message that they will act the way you want, but you can almost guarantee that unless your message is received and interpreted the way that you intended, the likelihood of your audience doing what you want is small. Selecting the right media is integral to creating complete communication, understanding, and cooperation.

Media Richness Level Details

Every communication will involve some type of media to transfer a message from the sender to the receiver. Typical communication media include e-mail, fax, telephone, video teleconferencing, face-to-face meeting, and group meeting, to name a few, and each of these media offers a different level of communication richness. Recall that when we talk about media richness, we are not talking about the speed or bandwidth of the physical channel, such as the megabit per second of transmission capability. Instead, we are talking about richness level as a blend of information and feedback availability, the timeliness of the feedback, and the level of information contained within the feedback.

COMMUNICATION COMPONENTS DIAGRAM

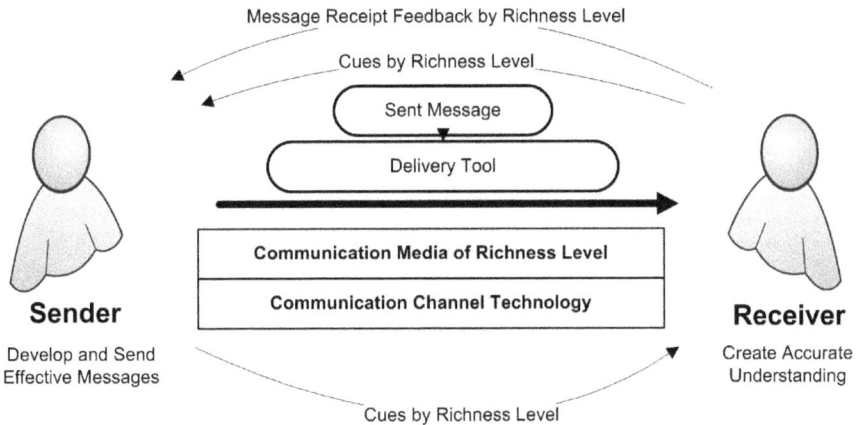

Message Receipt Feedback by Richness Level

Cues by Richness Level

Sent Message

Delivery Tool

Communication Media of Richness Level

Communication Channel Technology

Sender

Develop and Send
Effective Messages

Receiver

Create Accurate
Understanding

Cues by Richness Level

Today's communication environment has a wide variety of media. Let's take a moment to look in detail at how feedback and information transfer contribute to the media richness level. Assume that you received a text message from someone that reads, "I'm really looking forward to working out this evening." This phrasing in written form would indicate that the sending party is looking forward to exercising. Seems simple. Assume now that you are talking to that person on the telephone, and they say these same words with a different inflection on the words such as, "I am really (with strong, sarcastic inflection on "really") looking forward to working out this evening." Notice that the spoken words are the same as those written in the text but the strong, sarcastic inflection on the word "really" changes the message from one of enthusiasm about working out to one indicating a lack of enthusiasm. This shift in understanding was communicated by a simple change in vocal inflection on one word, which we will call a *cue*. That inflection would have been completely lost, or more accurately unavailable, in an email, text, or written letter. This added level of information-carrying capability, which offers additional cues such as inflection, makes vocal communication a richer form of communication than text.

Now assume that you are looking at the person while having the conversation. Assume that, in this case, they say, "I am really looking forward to working out this evening," but when they say, "Really," they roll their eyes up and to the right. Notice that the words again are identical to those in the text message, and the person's vocal inflection may have been neutral, but the visual action of moving their eyes around indicates sarcasm in a way that was not available with either the written or telephone communication methods. Adding the visual cue component to the communication offered another level of information richness to the communication, thus making face-to-face communication richer than telephone communication. Media richness is based on the ability of a media to transfer information and feedback between sender and receiver in such a way that it affects message interpretation. The eye roll was a visual cue that was immediately received, which makes face-to-face very rich. The email and text lack vocal inflection or visual cues, so they are relatively much leaner.

As another example, let's consider a paper letter sent by a woman in the United States to a serviceman stationed overseas. Notice that the paper form of communication is very lean in that feedback is limited and highly delayed (a return letter is called "snail mail" for a reason), and the message can contain only what is in the envelope. Now assume that instead of typing the letter on plain white paper, she sends the letter using high-quality bond paper and hand writes the note. These simple changes personalize the letter changing its significance (information level) to the receiver. Now assume that she places a few drops of perfume on the bond paper before putting it into the envelope. I can promise you that the serviceman will have a completely different interpretation of the perfumed letter compared to the more sterile typed letter on white paper. (Personal experience is talking with this example.) Even a lean form of communication, such as a written paper letter, can carry a more significant message with the addition of quality bond paper, a handwritten message, and a couple of drops of perfume. But, it can be made richer only within the limitations of the lean media level used, which still suffers from feedback and timing limitations. Increased media richness offers increased feedback and information transfer potential between receiver and sender.

Do you recall our earlier discussion about the problematic role communication barriers play when fostering complete communication? Feedback is a key ingredient for minimizing the impact of these barriers. Timely feedback allows the sender to determine the level of received message understanding. The benefit of this is that should the sender believe that the message was not received as intended, she can quickly ask for clarification from the receiver and adjust the message to address that misunderstanding. Remember steps 2 and 3 of the complete communication model? Without feedback, the sender might never know that the message was not received as intended. Even more troubling is the very real possibility that without feedback, the sender will expect that the receiver understood the message as intended and interpret subsequent receiver actions in that context. This initial misunderstanding offers perilous ground for misinterpretation of future messages and can cause problems that could have been avoided with a properly confirmed initial communication.

Proactively determining the level of richness needed to verify accurate message receipt is critical to best ensure that your messages are understood as intended. The required richness level is determined by a combination of situational and audience characteristics, which are covered in later chapters. The Paulson Media Matching Method (presented in Chapter 6) offers a systematic approach for determining the level of richness and feedback needed for a given communication situation. The specific components of the matching method are presented in Chapters 4 and 5 and tied together in Chapter 6.

Additional Thoughts on Media Richness Levels and the Selection Process

It has been interesting to me to watch how we naturally tend to escalate richness levels as our level of uncertainty increases. We will discuss this topic in more detail in Chapter 4, which presents how situational characteristics affect richness level selection, and I thought a brief discussion would benefit us here as well.

Media characteristics that determine information richness

Informa-tion Rich-ness	Media	Feed-back	Source
High (5) (Very Rich)	Face-to-Face individual or group meetings, video-teleconference	Immedi-ate	Personal/full feedback
(4)	Telephone, audio tele-conference, voice mes-sage	Fast	Personal/voice-only feedback
(3)	E-mail, FAX, Text Mes-saging, Interactive Messaging	Slower	Personal/text only
(2)	Written Personal Note, Written Personal Memo	Very Slow	Personal/time restrict-ed
Low (1) (Very Lean)	Report Written, Report Numeric, Written General Memo, Written General Broadcast Letter	Very Slow and Unlikely	Impersonal: "To whom it may concern ...."

Note: Based on Daft & Lengel,[1] Rice[2] published works and Paulson's experience.

Assume that a written business letter containing an important message is sent through the standard postal service. The sender writes a paper letter paying close attention to personalize the letter for the intended receiver before dropping it into the mailbox with the belief that it will find the intended receiver. First, notice that the sender may not even know if the letter was physically received. The Post Office created its return receipt service to offer feedback on this uncertainty. Should the sender not receive a confirmation response within what he feels is a reasonable timeframe, he will likely send a confirmation e-mail to the receiver, telephone the receiver, or physically visit the receiver. The sender who does not receive a reply will likely choose to increase the richness level by several levels over the initial lean level in his quest for feedback. Most of us would have followed a similar richness escalation procedure, especially if there was a high level of perceived risk in our minds associated with the letter not being interpreted as we had intended. Risk is an important and often overlooked communication characteristic and is covered in a later Chapter 5: Audience Considerations.

Feedback using e-mail is more real-time than paper mail in that an email can be received within seconds of when it was sent, enabling the receiver to reply quickly. We all know that this is how email works. But even with all of this speedy communication capability, should the receiver choose not to respond, the sender is still in the dark related to how the received message was interpreted or whether it was received at all. How many of us have missed an important email because it was automatically moved to our Spam folder? The sender would not know this. There is no feedback unless initiated by the receiver, so email is still considered leaner communication media.

A face-to-face meeting is high in richness. The parties can see each other. They can hear each other's voices. They can view body language, smell the room, and shake hands. A full range of sensory feedback possibilities is available face-to-face that are simply not available with leaner media. There are some who believe that due to its high richness level, a face-to-face meeting is the ideal communication mode for most, if not all, messages. This is not accurate, and using rich media to communicate in a simple situation can create misunderstandings, as we will see in the following example. Plus, face-to-face meetings are arguably the most expensive from a time and resource perspective, and using meetings inefficiently can be costly both financially and with lost morale.

StreetSmarts

There is a lot of post-pandemic discussion about whether folks should be returning to the office or not. There are functional ways to determine whether someone can do their job remotely as well, if not better, than in the office with others. The same considerations presented in the Paulson Media Matching Method (Chapter Six) can be applied to the working face-to-face or remote decision. Remember, all tasks and situations are not the same and can be done with varying media richness levels, which means that an investigation into the media needed to perform the bulk of a person's function would determine whether they should be in-house or remote. Book Three in the book series "Flexibly Tough" will discuss organizational design based on communication which includes the application of media richness to job definition and remote work decisions.

Assume that for the first time in months, your boss stops you in the hall and asks that you stop by her office in an hour without giving a reason. You ask what it is about, and she says something like, "Oh, nothing. We can talk about it when you get there." What would go through your head? Is something wrong? What could she want to talk about? Are you going to be part of the recent layoffs? You might even ask co-workers if this has ever happened to them before. In other words, you might spend the next hour doing nothing but thinking about the reason for the meeting. When you arrive at the meeting, your boss sits you down and says that she has a new phone extension and wants to make sure you have it. That is it. Nothing more than a simple phone extension update, and she ends the meeting. Now, what goes through your head? Why would she call a meeting for something so simple that could have been in an email? What else was she looking for? You might even get a little annoyed that she wasted so much of your time on such a simple message. All this extra stuff goes on in the background of what would have otherwise been a simple communication. Notice how using rich communication for everything is not an effective solution because using rich communication when not warranted not only wastes valuable personnel time but can also cause unnecessary confusion.

Interactive live/in-person group meetings present an interesting richness evaluation situation. All the visual, audio, and sensory feedback cues of an individual face-to-face meeting are available to all participants, which means that each meeting attendee can send and receive cues from any of the other attendees. This also means that the number of cue paths grows geometrically with the number of meeting attendees making the interactive in-person group meeting arguably the richest form of communication available today.

A group presentation where the audience listens to a single speaker is different from an interactive group meeting in that the interaction is substantially limited to between the speaker and the attendees, with little interaction happening between the audience members themselves. There may be a lot of people in the room at the same time, but the level of interaction is constrained by the nature of the communication venue, so it would not be considered as rich as a face-to-face individual or interactive group meeting.

The "Source" column of the table warrants a few words in that it credits richness to the level of personal involvement by the sender with the communication. A paper-form letter uses the paper on which it is written as the source of the communication and may have been written by a computer program. This is about as impersonal as you can get. When a person writes a letter, it is more personal, but the message is still being delivered by a piece of paper which is still impersonal. Email falls into this category as well in that a person types the email, but it is being delivered by a computer screen and not the person. A face-to-face meeting, on the other hand, uses the sender himself as the source of the communication, so it is personal. The telephone call or an audio teleconference is still personal in that the person's voice is delivering the message.

StreetSmarts

A group presentation scenario is analogous to what happens in a typical video teleconference meeting using a product like GoToMeeting or Zoom. As attendees, we are one person looking at a group of faces on a screen, but there is minimal attendee-to-attendee interaction except for what might be happening using the private chat feature. Even then, this is a major limitation for online group meetings compared to face-to-face group meetings, and this spontaneous inter-member interaction limitation will need to be solved before online meetings can genuinely replace the conventional face-to-face group meeting. This is a strong argument for expecting all who attend a video conference to have their camera's on to offer as much richness as possible from the media.

E-mail, text messaging, interactive messaging, personal letters, and personal memos can be thought of as personal in nature in that they are specific, one-on-one communication between two unique parties, and some level of personal information must have been provided for the communication to occur. You cannot text message someone unless he has offered you his cellular phone number. When you communicate using text messaging, you assume that you are communicating directly with the other party on a somewhat personal, real-time basis. But you still cannot hear or see him, which precludes verbal and visual interaction, and feedback is limited, which keeps this media still relatively lean. It is so lean that there is no way to confirm that the intended person is actually replying to the texts. It could be someone else using their phone.

Shift Your Media Richness Selection from Automatic to Conscious

A fundamental premise of Outcome Oriented Communication and the Paulson Media Matching Method is that the communication method you choose should not be based primarily on convenience or reflex: it should be based on the specifics of a given communication situation and your desired outcomes. Ask businesspeople how they choose communication media, and most will tell you that they choose the media based on convenience ("to get it off my desk") or based on what is most commonly used within their organization. A common approach is that people respond to a message using the same communication media type over which they received a message without considering if that media richness is correct for their reply. For example, if you've received an e-mail, your first inclination would be to respond using e-mail, even though the content of the message and the circumstances of the communication environment might lend themselves better to a different, richer communication media. Instead of considering the most effective method of communication response, most people click "Reply" (the most expedient) and send their e-mail response. For many, if email is their reflexive media of communication, they respond to everything with an email. Think about all the unwanted "Reply All" messages you have received to convince yourself that people often reply reflexively.

As another example, if somebody calls and leaves a message on your voice message box, your natural inclination may be to use the telephone to call them back, often having to leave a voice message yourself. Or, if email is your reflexive communication method, you might simply respond to the voice message using email. This might be easiest or most common, but it is very possibly not the form of communication most likely to help you achieve your communication outcome. In fact, using a form of communication that is low in richness, such as email, when dealing with complex communication situations can complicate them in ways that would not have occurred if a more appropriate richer media type had been used. Not selecting the proper media when responding to a communication situation can complicate what would otherwise have been simple.

Chapter Summary

Media richness theory differentiated the speed of a communication channel from the richness of the information communicated over that channel between senders and receivers. It offered a structured way of selecting the proper communication media for a given communication situation. A key aspect of complete communication involves feedback between a sender and a receiver. Media richness theory incorporated feedback as a key media selection consideration. This chapter introduced several key concepts that serve as the foundation for the Paulson Media Matching Method. Learning how to apply the concepts presented in this chapter will greatly improve your communication effectiveness in our diverse, media-intensive world. The following chapters add situational and personal considerations which are related to communication filters. These filters drive the media richness selection process and enable you to use a more comprehensive approach to creating complete communication and achieving your intended communication outcomes.

CHAPTER FOUR

Evaluating The Communication Situation

Creating successful outcomes within an organization requires that tasks performed by various people combine to create the intended outcome. With each step along the way, someone will communicate with another worker in some way to convince that person to cooperate with achieving the intended outcome. It is important to remember that organizations are made up of people with varied backgrounds, personalities, and motivations which complicates the communication environment. Creating repeatable communication and business success through a wide variety of people is dependent upon understanding the complexity of the work to be accomplished, the organizational environment within that work must occur, and the people through which the success is accomplished. You can only be a successful leader if your communication creates the perception in the mind of your audience that they should support you, which is done through a combination of message creation and message delivery. Yes … becoming an effective communicator takes work, but it also takes a framework for understanding.

When selecting the best media to use for sending a message, you must consider the specific task characteristics as well as environmental (i.e., cultural) influences at play within the organization where the communication takes place. You can think of these as the influences imposed on the task or situation by the surrounding environment and are related to the Paulson Media Matching Method chart section labeled "Chapter 4: Situational Factors". By the end of this chapter, you will have a better understanding of *task complexity, organizational complexity, information required,* and *outcome predictability* and the role they play in media selection.

Chapter 5 looks at the audience-related aspects of communication. Both are intended to give you a better understanding of the communication filters that influence message creation, communication receptiveness, and media richness level selection, which combined establish their willingness to cooperate with you, which is ultimately what you are trying to create.

Task Complexity, Information Requirements, and Routineness

Have you ever sent an email to someone that you carefully crafted for clarity, only to have them reply that they didn't have a clue what you were talking about? Or had a meeting about a complex topic only to have others in the meeting tell you that they wish they had known where the meeting was going so that they could have brought their engineers to interpret? If so, then I feel your pain. It has happened to all of us. There is a reasonable chance that you assumed, incorrectly or unconsciously, that your audience knew as much about your topic as you did, and when that turned out not to be true, you created miscommunication and all of the emotional fallout that comes with it.

It turns out that selecting the correct media richness level for communication related to a specific task or situation is related in part to the level of complexity of the topic/task being discussed and the experience level of the person responsible for the topic/task. From this relationship of task complexity and worker experience, we can determine what we will call the *routineness* of a communication situation from which we can select the proper media richness level for your message delivery. In other words, you don't start communication with an email or phone call. Instead, you start by evaluating the situation or task under consideration in combination with the information or knowledge needed to successfully complete the task, then relate these to the experience level of the person charged with completing the task. This combination allows you to determine the routineness of the task or situation, which then allows you to determine the best media richness level for sending your message. Are you now starting to see why reflexively replying to an email is not the best media selection approach? Take a breath. This may all sound like a lot to consider, but after you make this conceptual shift, you can never go back, which is a good thing!

These abstract concepts are practically applied when matching the right person to the right job supported by the right communication framework, which is the topic of Book 3, "Flexibly Tough: Building Resilient Organizations using Communication," so I won't cover the details here. But some core concepts are needed to help us with media selection, the topic of this book. If you take the time to understand what follows, your relationship with tasks and the workers who perform them will change for the better. Now, let's take a closer look at task complexity, information, worker experience, routiness, and media richness.

Task Complexity and Critical Thinking

When workers perform their work, they process information in some form, determine how that information applies to their current situation, and then they choose a course of action. The more efficiently workers complete this sequence to a successful outcome, the more successful the organization will be. The complexity level of the worker's task is related to the level of *critical thinking* needed to perform the task.

Definition

Critical thinking is the process of evaluating information from various viewpoints to determine a course of action. This typically involves some type of information search and analysis process which will be done using some type of communication media such as a handbook or an online knowledgebase lookup.

A *novice* is a person with little to no experience related to a specific topic area.

An *expert* is someone with much experience related to a specific topic area.

Routineness is related to the level of complexity of a task, the level of information needed to complete the task, the level of critical thinking involved with analyzing the information, and the specific experience of the involved worker assigned to complete the task.

Response uncertainty is the response by a novice worker to do nothing when faced with an overwhelmingly complex situation.

An *ambiguous* situation is one where all pertinent information related to the decision is available to the decision maker, experts may offer conflicting opinions, and the best course of action remains unclear.

Task Complexity ranges from *Simple* to *Complicated*. A simple task is one where completing the task relies upon information that is easily found and analyzed and requires a low level of worker critical thinking to determine the next action. An example of this would be one where a worker reads a gauge on a piece of machinery, looks up the reading in a reference manual, and then takes the actions specified in the manual. The information required is easily understood (unequivocal), and the proper actions are clearly defined and easily accomplished. The level of training or experience needed to understand and complete this simple task is low.

A complicated task is one where the information required is not readily available or clear (equivocal) or must be cross-referenced with other information to determine its significance, all of which require a much higher level of worker critical thinking. An example of this would be a situation where the same worker from before records readings on three different gauges that, when referenced in the manual, require actions that conflict with each other. What is the worker to do? He can see something is not normal from the gauge readings, but the reference manual instructions for this situation are not clear. He must determine, on his own, the proper next step. Can you see how the level of critical thinking has increased? This is the type of situation that we often read about after the fact, where a worker knew something was wrong but did not escalate it to the required levels for remediation before it became a disaster. They took the wrong initiative on their own (or possibly did nothing) because they did not have the knowledge to determine the best next step. You will see that a complicated task is best given to an experienced person who will be able to "figure out" the best next step.

Routineness Related to Worker Experience Relationship

The prior explanation is based in part on the work of Charles Perrow[1,] who proposed an approach for matching people to tasks. We will refer to inexperienced workers as *novices* and very experienced workers as *experts*. His rationale was that the novice worker doesn't have the conceptual framework for resolving a complex task. The novice presented with a complex situation might experience *response uncertainty* whereby that person is unable to adequately understand the task so that a viable course of action can be determined. It is common for a novice worker to not fully understand a situation's complexity and, as a result, not realize that the situation's success is in jeopardy until it is too late. An expert worker is more likely to recognize a problem early and to know how to address it, better ensuring successful analysis and remediation. He called a simple situation *routine* and a complex one *non-routine*. We care about routineness because it is used to determine the richness level of the media that is best for a given communication. We will also talk about an extremely non-routine situation as *ambiguous*. This is one where no additional information can be applied to finding a solution. Ambiguity is such an important topic that a later section in this chapter is dedicated to its discussion. A detailed discussion of worker experience is presented in Chapter 5.

MATCHING OF COMPLEXITY TO WORKER EXPERIENCE LEVEL

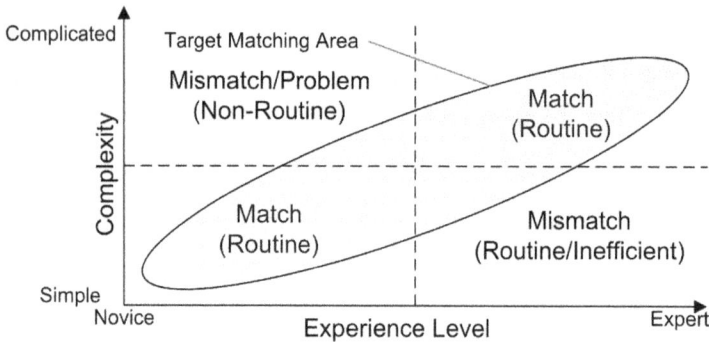

The chart graphically represents the matching relationship of complexity to worker experience. The horizontal axis shows the *Experience* level of the worker from *Novice* on the left to *Expert* on the right. The vertical axis shows *Task Complexity* from *Simple* at the bottom to *Complicated* at the top. The upper left quadrant shows a potentially serious mismatch because a complicated situation was assigned to a novice employee, making it non-routine, which can jeopardize a project if this task is mission-critical. Remember our gauge reader with conflicting data? These are the mismatches that can hurt you. The lower right quadrant represents a mismatch because an experienced person is assigned a simple task. This mismatch will not jeopardize a project because the task will be seen as routine to the worker, but if it happens often, it indicates your experienced people are being underutilized and how they are being used is inefficient. The lower left quadrant shows a good match because an inexperienced person is assigned a simple task, making it routine for that worker. The upper right quadrant shows a good match with an experienced person assigned to a complicated task which for them will likely be routine.

The prior discussion was needed to help you determine the routiness level of a task or situation, which is needed to select the proper media richness level. A major wrinkle in evaluating routineness is that a given situation might be perceived as non-routine by a novice person (everything is new) but appear routine to a more experienced person who has previously handled similar situations. In other words, a person's experience strongly influences the person's routineness perception. This means that a situation's routineness cannot fully be evaluated without considering the experience level of the persons involved, which is why a section of Chapter 5 is dedicated to evaluating experience.

Relating Routiness to Media Richness

The work of Daft and Lengel[2] that introduced media richness theory showed that richer media should be used when workers were processing more equivocal (uncertain) information and that leaner media worked well when processing less equivocal (more certain) information. They wrote that evaluating uncertain information required a higher level of critical thinking which sounds a lot like Perrow. Linking the two, we can say that a situation that is less complex with clearer information is a routine one (less critical thinking), and a more complex situation with less clear information is non-routine (more critical thinking). We can now relate media richness to routineness. The chart graphically represents the relationship.

MATCHING OF ROUTINENESS TO MEDIA RICHNESS

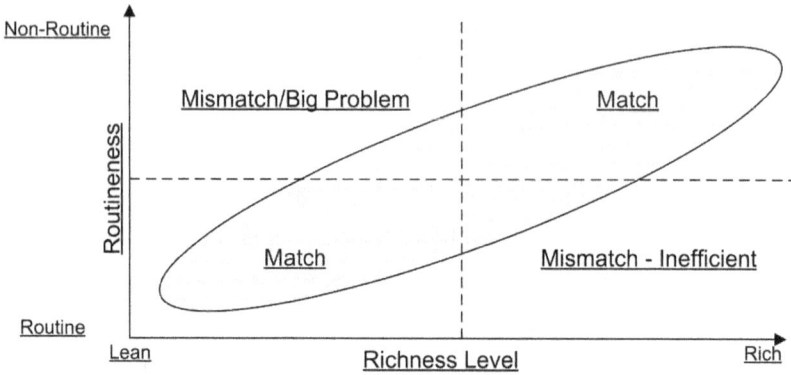

Non-Routine

Routineness

Mismatch/Big Problem | Match

Match | Mismatch - Inefficient

Routine

Lean | Richness Level | Rich

The chart's horizontal axis represents media richness, with Lean media on the left and Rich media on the right. The vertical axis shows Routineness with Routine at the bottom and Non-Routine at the top. The lower left shows a match because we are using a lean media to convey a routine topic, such as a phone number change. The upper right shows a match in that we are using a rich media to communicate about a non-routine topic such as organizational restructuring. The upper left quadrant shows a mismatch because we used lean media to deal with a non-routine communication situation, such as conveying a layoff notice. The lower right shows a mismatch because we are using rich media to discuss a routine topic, such as changing a contact phone number. Notice that the lower left and upper right quadrants are again matches. I can tell you that in my over 30 years of applying this media matching approach in working situations that it is correct most of the time.

We had to take a circuitous route to show the functional relationship of routineness to media richness, but I thought it important for you to understand the rationale behind determining a situation's routineness level. It is not obvious, and most of us learn this reality by trial and error. Using the framework described here, you now have a systematic way of determining a situation's routiness and can confidently select the best media richness for delivering your message.

Media Matching Bottom Line About Routineness: Lean media richness is appropriate for communicating routine information for routine circumstances, and richer media should be used for communicating non-routine information for more non-routine circumstances. Remember that routineness is determined by a combination of the complexity of the task or situation, the clarity of involved information, and the experience of the persons involved. It is necessary to consider all of this to determine the routineness of the situation from which you can determine the best media richness level for message delivery.

Organizational Complexity Considerations

A corporation may be a legal entity that has the legal right to transact business, but a corporation without people would get nothing done. People give an organization its life, its direction, its unique talents, and its unique foibles. Any time you get people involved in a situation, you add a fluid level of interpersonal complexity. I think of the corporation as the legal framework within which people work, but I look at the people as the reason why the corporation exists in the first place. Outcome Oriented Communication is essentially about evaluating an organizational situation from an interpersonal communication perspective so that your specific outcomes can be accomplished. Things get accomplished, and outcomes are achieved through the people who work for the corporation, which means that any communication approach must start with the persons involved. Book Two, "Getting Agreement: Designing Messages That Create Cooperation," provides an approach for evaluating a communication situation within the context of the overall organization, its culture, and personnel so that you construct messages most likely to get agreement and cooperation.

Whenever people are involved, an organization becomes complex, and depending on the organizational culture, this complexity can be constructive or destructive. As an example, let's take something as routine as a salesperson completing and submitting an expense report form. This seems simple, but it can become complex if the clerical support person who processes the reimbursement request does not like our salesperson and chooses to continually put his completed expense report form at the bottom of the stack. The result is that the reimbursement form is slow to get processed, the salesperson gets upset because the company is slow in repaying business-related travel expenses, and the accounting team gets upset with the salesperson for not keeping up on his expenses, creating ill will all around. The sad part is that all of this could have been avoided had the clerical support person simply processed the form in accordance with company procedures. But this person, for personal reasons, chose to stall the form submission, thus creating unnecessary complexity and perhaps distrust among many people. With people comes uncertainty and complexity. You care about this because a person's communication filters are tuned to be receptive or not based on how they perceive the person sending the message.

Some level of organizational complexity will always be present when dealing with people, and for this reason, complexity is evaluated as part of the media matching process. Complexity should be evaluated from three perspectives: political influences, interpersonal relationships, and intergroup interaction. In this context, think of political influences being those that involve the self-serving interests of a given person or group. When political matters are involved, selfless actions should not be expected unless the apparently "selfless" person will somehow benefit in a self-serving way. This may be difficult to deal with if you are the person working with the politically motivated person, but if you understand the situation correctly, you are on better footing to handle it. Situations where the involved parties share common goals and ultimate outcomes should be considered simple.

Situations involving a strong political component will typically have one party working strongly for his own benefit over that of others and are generally complex to navigate. Interpersonal relationships will always involve the personalities of the sender and receiver, making interpersonal relationship evaluation important. When the relationship is cooperative, the situational complexity is simple, and the communication filters are less likely to negatively impact message receipt. But when the relationship is hostile or unpredictable in some way, it should be considered complex with a high likelihood of message misinterpretation.

A group can have a personality that is distinct from that of the individual group members, and sometimes group thinking will influence persons to act in ways that are contrary to their natural, individual personal inclination. As with individuals, if intergroup communication is typically cooperative, then the interpersonal situation can be considered simple. But, if intergroup communication is often hostile or unpredictable, then it should be considered complex.

Daft and Lenge[2] provided a conceptual construct that explained the relationship between information richness and complexity of organizational phenomenon. They contended that less complex organizational situations (*Routine*) required a leaner communication media and that more complex organizational phenomena (*Non-routine*) required a richer communication media. They reported that using mismatched communication media for a specific organizational situation can create problems instead of solve them.

Recall that one key aspect of richer media is the quick availability of feedback to allow you, as the sender, to evaluate your audience's reaction to your message. If the reaction does not match what you intended and you would categorize the audience as unfriendly, there is a high likelihood that their "unfriendly" filters shaded the message into something you did not intend. The richer media feedback enabled you to know this and potentially adjust the message to ensure accurate receipt. If the same message were sent with an email, you could have an inaccurately interpreted message floating around in your company, doing damage that would be unseen to you.

For example, using a lean communication media such as a form letter to communicate a complex organizational phenomenon like a layoff provides too few clues between sender and receiver, is impersonal, and offers no feedback mechanism. This would explain the notorious reputation of the layoff *"pink slip."* A person who receives a "pink slip" informing them that they have lost their job quite often will say something like, "The least they could have done is told me to my face!" In essence, the recipient immediately wanted a richer form of communication for the delivery of the message so that additional information such as vocal inflection, body language, and visual appearance could help them with processing the impact of what is a non-routine situation to them. On the other hand, using a rich communication media such as a face-to-face meeting for a low-complexity organizational problem such as a change of telephone number can create unintended ambiguity by providing too many cues to the message recipient. When people are specifically asked to participate in a rich communication about a simple information item, they often wonder, "What else was going on?" or "What did I miss?" A simple e-mail message (leaner richness level) would have adequately delivered the phone number change message with minimal likelihood of misunderstanding. The rich media selection (a meeting) for a simple message leaves the receiver wondering about the message far beyond the meeting.

Media Matching Bottom Line About Organizational Complexity: Complex organizational situations are typically best addressed using a richer form of communication, whereas leaner communication might be adequate for simpler organizational situations.

Information Requirements, Certainty, and Ambiguity

We have talked a lot about the importance of information clarity in setting the level of required critical thinking and routineness, so it felt like a few words about certainty and ambiguity was warranted. A definition of uncertainty is the difference between the amount of information required to perform the task and the amount of information already possessed by the organization[3]. In other words, if more information offers clarity, then the situation is uncertain. This definition implies that when we remove enough information uncertainty by getting answers to questions, a reliable (certain) course of action can be determined. Hidden in this definition is the tacit assumption that when we label something "uncertain," we expect that additional information is available somewhere, and it is only a matter of finding it. As more information is obtained, the more certain the situation and course of action become. Uncertain situations enable managers and workers to ask questions, get answers to those questions, and analyze those answers to determine viable tasks and actions. It may be possible to accomplish this using lean media, such as email, if the situation appears routine to the involved parties.

Ambiguous situations, on the other hand, are ill-defined and often give rise to multiple interpretations by experienced parties who view the same situational symptoms. Ambiguous situations may give rise to confusion, disagreement, and misunderstanding on the part of responsible personnel. No amount of information will clear up an ambiguous situation, which makes it different from an uncertain situation. There is likely no standardized method or set of rules for addressing an ambiguous situation which means that it will require a high level of critical thinking. The final course of action will be determined by workers based on their personal experience and knowledge and not on procedures found in a company manual. Those involved will need to actively interact to determine a course of action that calls for them to have access to the most possible communication cues and the quickest possible feedback. In other words, level 4 or 5 richness is needed.

65

StreetSmarts

At the time of this writing, there is a raging debate about the future of the Earth with respect to the causes of global warming. One group of scientists is looking at the available information and believes that the Earth is on a troubling course towards increased global warming due to man-made pollutants and predicts profoundly negative future outcomes. Another group of scientists is looking at the same information and saying that the Earth is naturally warming due to a natural global cycle, and that is not the result of man-made pollutants. The first group is pushing hard for changes to pollution regulations in the belief that reducing pollutants will improve the future. The second group is not supportive of these new regulations because they would unnecessarily harm the economy and would not make a difference anyway. This is an ambiguous situation in that seasoned experts are looking at the same information and arriving at different conclusions. As time unfolds, we will gain more information that may tip the scales one way or the other, but given the information we have today, we are stuck with ambiguity.

When faced with an ambiguous situation, managers and workers may not know what questions to ask and have no established rule book to follow. Ambiguous situations are not easily addressed by more information because there might be no clear agreement about the types of additional information that would help address the situation. The BP oil spill in the Gulf of Mexico in 2010 could be considered an ambiguous situation in that an accident of this nature had never occurred at this depth before, and there was much disagreement as to the right way to evaluate or address the situation. There wasn't even agreement as to the severity of the problem.[4] Anyone who followed the news reports associated with the spill will recall the number of false starts, the increasing disagreement about the level of damage, and the struggles that officials had in keeping the public informed about a situation that was not well understood. As key new information surfaced, the context of the situation would change, as would the proposed best remediation methods. There was no obvious "right" answer to the problem as it was happening, or it would have been more easily and quickly corrected. This could arguably be viewed as an uncertain situation in that more information in the hands of the right people might have caused a different result, but for those on the site, it was ambiguous.

Media Matching Bottom Line About Uncertainty and Ambiguity: Certain situations and information, such as the weekend weather, can be communicated using lean media because most message recipients will interpret the weather report in a similar way. Uncertain situations will usually require richer media so that the message recipients can interact to determine the significance of the information. Ambiguous situations should always be addressed with richer forms of media.

Final Outcome Certainty Assessment

Intuition is a powerful barometer and, in many ways, more insightful than the most sophisticated analysis. If your analysis tells you that a situation is routine, but your intuition tells you that the likelihood of you achieving your communication outcome is unpredictable, then look for incorrect assumptions related to personnel experience, routineness, communication richness, or information clarity. Correcting these mismatches will likely move your intuition toward more predictability. If you find no mismatches, but you still have low outcome predictability, then ask yourself, what do you not know? Your intuition is hesitant for a reason, and taking another look at what you think you know will often bring incorrect assumptions to light.

If you move forward with your intuition on alert, look for ways that you can use richer communication media and more experienced personnel to monitor developments. That way, you will have feedback as things unfold that will often explain the reasons for your intuitive concerns. It is likely something that you don't know consciously, but your intuition picked up on.[5]

On the other hand, should your intuition tell you that everything is fine and outcome success is highly predictable, but the analysis shows communication richness mismatches that are outside of your control, then you would be well advised to add insurance by compensating for the mismatches or at least monitoring to see if progress matches your intuition.

StreetSmarts

A valuable aspect of using a communication model is that it can also act as a diagnostic tool to determine what is missing should your communication not work as intended. You are learning a media matching approach that is designed to help you determine the proper level of media richness for a given communication situation, with the intent that your message be clearly understood as you intended. Should you follow the method guidelines and not get the intended communication results, then you can use the model to help you determine what you missed. Perhaps you assumed experience in an area that your audience does not actually have? Or perhaps you assumed that your audience is part of a simple organizational culture when it is actually very complex? If you did not get the result you expected, then go back and review your assumptions against the media matching model to determine what you might have missed or gotten incorrect. I have used this approach countless times, and it works.

Media Matching Bottom Line About Outcome Certainty: If your analysis of a communication situation offers you a high predictability of achieving your desired communication outcome, and your intuition concurs, then move forward as planned. If your outcome predictability analysis level is high, but your intuition does not agree, then re-analyze the factors and see if you missed anything. If not, then lean toward richer media to either allow you to become more certain or to uncover through feedback what is missing, so you adjust for incorrect assumptions before they become a problem.

Chapter Summary

We covered a lot of conceptual ground in this chapter. It is difficult to overstate the importance of a complete understanding of the relationship of your audience to the topic of your communication. Are they experienced with the topic? With your company? With you? With the industry? With the technology? It is also critical to evaluate the certainty of the information used to inform you and your audience. Is there a consensus on the information and its significance, or is there disagreement? Remember that all these things affect the filters through which they will understand the message you send. The more likely they are to misunderstand you, the richer the form of media you should use. Only by receiving the feedback offered by rich media can you quickly know that there is a misunderstanding and take steps to correct it. Your goal with communication is always to ensure that the message you send is received by your audience as you intended. Selecting the right media richness level is integral to ensuring message receipt success, and before you can select the media, you need to determine the routineness of the message, which is related to the experience of your audience. Taking the time in advance to evaluate these important topics will minimize your need to do communication "damage control" in the future.

Understanding The Audience

As I have mentioned many times, your desired communication results cannot be achieved without the cooperation of the receiver of your communication - the audience. Given the importance of the audience in achieving your desired outcomes, it makes the most sense to construct communication messages so that they will elicit the desired audience response. The more you understand about your audience, the more informed you will be when constructing messages, selecting media, and designing the details associated with a delivery package, such as an email, presentation, or meeting. Recall that all communication involves filters for both the sender and the receiver, and a key goal is to construct the communication such that the filters do not become barriers.

One key filter component is the experience of your audience, which we talked about in some detail in Chapter 4. In this chapter, we will offer a rationale for why experience is so important, and you will see that it is not general experience, but specific experience, that is important to consider. We also talked briefly in Chapter 4 about how audience perception affects filters, and this topic is looked at more deeply here. The influence of culture on filter tuning cannot be over-emphasized, and it is also discussed in this chapter. A final and very important topic related to media selection is the Perceived Risk level of either the message sender or receiver. You will see that as Perceived Risk increases, the likelihood of miscommunication also increases, and Perceived Risk is so important that it can override all other considerations when selecting the right media richness. Topics in this chapter are included in the "Audience Profile" section of the Paulson Media Matching Method chart.

Audiences are complex, and these complexities can overshadow the rest of your communication planning excellence if not considered as part of a comprehensive communication approach.

Experience Changes the Way We Think

There is a solid body of research that supports the premise that people with much experience with a given situation typically view that situation differently and with greater insight than those who are inexperienced. They may remember more details, see more interrelationships, and see more potential avenues of approach than more novice persons. One possible explanation for this difference is that their more extensive experience base offers an existing background memory foundation that reduces demands on working foreground (cognitive) memory and frees more working memory to interpret the unique situation immediately before them.[1] For example, experts may store more models in their memory and establish more linkages between the models than novices, leading to more complete activation between linked models and knowledge retrieval.[2] For a detailed and interesting discussion about the associative nature of the brain and its ability to store and process information, check out *Brain Bugs.*[3]

One researcher performed a multi-year case study of an information analyst from the securities industry to evaluate his perceptions of task complexity over time. Early in the subject's career, he perceived more tasks as complex, whereas later, as an expert, he found fewer tasks complex. The study supported the premise that the same tasks will be seen as more or less complex as a direct result of the worker's experience.[4]

Other research has indicated that business knowledge, technical knowledge, product knowledge, company-specific (institutional) knowledge, cultural knowledge, and project management knowledge were important for successfully managing projects,[5] and that complex environments and problems require the exploitation of more types of knowledge.[6]

One project management expert suggested that five areas of worker experience should be considered when evaluating IT project personnel: experience with the technology, experience with the worker's company (the employer), experience with the project team personnel, experience with the end user's company, and experience with the end user's industry. He defined an experienced worker as one that had worked on only one prior project involving the area in question. For example, if a worker had worked on a single project using a specific technology, that worker would be considered experienced with that technology.[7] I used to think that a single experience was not enough, but over the years, I have changed my mind. In watching novices perform tasks, I have seen that the level of knowledge they possess after only a single experience is much higher than when they had no experience, and the way that they approach the next similar occurrence, their level of critical thinking is more advanced.

So, I concur with the importance of experience in these areas but also believe that certain of these experience areas will have greater relevance for certain project tasks than for others and are not equally relevant to all tasks in all project phases. For example, customer and employer experience will usually be more pertinent when addressing customer service dissatisfaction issues. Technical and team experience would be more pertinent when efficiently and responsibly addressing a complicated technical problem. *Technology* should not only be thought of as something involving 1s and 0s. It should be thought of as anything involving a specific methodology or other intellectual property that may or may not have a software or hardware base.

StreetSmarts

Remember that worker experience contributes to routineness determination and a routineness determination is needed to match media richness. You should use lean media for routine situations and your should use richer media for non-routine situations, if possible. Sometimes the circumstances will restrict your media choices to lean only, in which case you should be aware of the richness mismatch and take steps to compensate for the loss of feedback and cues. In this way, you may find out about miscommunications and correct them before they become ingrained in the perception of your audience.

The research literature offers many cases where personnel were key to project success at every level, along with instances where lack of technological experience, lack of customer experience, and lack of industry experience contributed to project challenges.[8]

The following sections offer my rationale for why it is important for you to consider these five areas of worker experience when planning your communication message as well as your media richness selection. If your audience would be considered a novice in any of these experience areas, then there is a high likelihood that your situation, which may appear routine on the surface, may actually be non-routine and require richer communication.

Company (Employer) Experience

Just as two people with the same credentials will have different personalities, so will two companies within the same industry. Each company has its own unique personality, which represents a composite of historical and current influences. These influences can be a result of influential personnel, such as the founders, or external influences, such as surviving a war, depression, or economic boom period. The perceptions, ethical standards, and procedures of an organization evolve over time as a melding of these various influences, and no two companies will have evolved in the same way. We will talk more about this in the culture section of this chapter.

For this reason, a highly experienced person within an industry or technology will still be inexperienced with respect to his new employer, and there will be a learning curve as this person becomes comfortable enough to allow his prior experience to be fully applied. It is almost like learning a new dialect of a language one speaks fluently. More than one highly qualified, highly intelligent person has failed miserably by going into a new culture and trying to impose his "way" on them. Others might be polite for a while, but eventually, the new person will meet with cultural resistance – not necessarily because he is wrong but because it is just so different from what they previously knew. Remember also that they also have no prior experience with him and, as such, have no trusted way of interpreting if his new way is better or not. They may only know that it is new and reflexively not support it, or worse, oppose it.

StreetSmarts

If you are outside the company selling into the company (your audience) and have never worked with them before, then you are a novice to the communication as well. Experience works on both sides of the communication. When I was managing national accounts, one of my customers had a lot of personnel turnover such that in a particular meeting, I was the most experienced person in the room related to what I was selling. It was strange to see my customer looking to me for guidance on what *they* should do next!

The new employee does not understand his employer's norms for dealing with situations which, in many ways, freezes their prior industry experience.

They likely know exactly what they would do if working for their prior employer. They just don't have the experience with their current employer to know the "right" solution to a situation. They are in a risky position simply due to the fact that they are new and folks will be watching them. This is where the risk aspect of media selection comes into play, as discussed later in this chapter. Notice that this person is inexperienced with respect to their company and perhaps with you as well, which would push toward richer communication.

Customer Experience

The need for customer experience becomes clear when we view the customer as the audience for your communication. The customer could be a business customer, such as someone looking to purchase a product or service from your company or an internal customer to whom your team offers an internal product or service. In either case, the customer will be listening with filters that are intrinsic to his environment and needs. The more experience you have with that customer, the more you will be able to analyze those filters and then select an appropriate message and media for your messages that will create the understanding that achieves the intended outcome.

Consider two national account sale situations (Customer A and Customer B) where you are working to sell a large data network. Customer A might be prone to deciding by consensus. Customer B might be prone to deciding based on the input of a single, influential individual. For Customer A, catering to the "boss" might be seen by the customer as counterproductive and not in alignment with their company's communal culture. If the purchase would involve a longer-term relationship with your company, this could cost you credibility and perhaps the sale. For Customer B, catering to the "boss" might be just the right approach because everyone knows that she is the boss. Period. This approach could indicate to the Customer B personnel that you understand the situation and could earn you the deal. My point here is that the same product in the same industry being sold to two different company cultures using the same approach could cost you one deal and earn you the other. By being more sensitive to, and adapting to, the internal characteristics of the respective customer, which would come from experience with that customer, you would increase the likelihood of getting both.

StreetSmarts

There is a saying that we tend to treat those closest to us the worst, and I think this may apply to organizations as well. When we are preparing for a meeting with a prospective customer, we will plan the event to ensure that the prospect's time is not wasted, think through their decision influencers, and evaluate their decision-making processes to put the odds of gaining their approval on our side. But, often, we do not invest similar amounts of time when meeting with our fellow employees. Does that make sense? Just because we work together doesn't mean that we share common goals and viewpoints. Having assumed that in my past experience has proven to be a mistake. Just as we plan to gain a prospect's agreement, so should we plan to gain the approval of our co-workers. Take caution to never take your familiarity with them for granted and always treat them with a high level of respect.

An internal customer situation would be analogous to the external customer situation presented earlier but with the additional complication of existing internal relationships. The management team of the internal customer will likely have some type of existing relationship with other personnel within the organization (perhaps with your managers) through which influence can be applied. This means that an internal communication could have implications and repercussions within the organization that go far beyond this particular transaction. Being sensitive to the internal aspects as well as the personality characteristics of the customer team, which is developed from experience with that team, will help you greatly in adapting the message and delivery as needed to achieve your desired outcome. (For more on organizational factors, take a look at Chapter 4.) If you are not familiar with your customer, then your situation could be considered non-routine and warrant richer communication in the early days. After a short period of time, you will have established communication norms with your customer, and moving to leaner media may be ok.

Dominant Technology Experience

Today's technologically dependent world is incredibly complex, and it is the rare person who has extensive experience across a wide range of technologies. Using digital technology as an example, someone highly experienced with programming databases might have little experience with network design and administration. A person who is highly experienced with network design may have limited experience with enterprise security policy development and implementation. None of these people may have extensive experience working with the computer hardware upon which the applications and networks run. In other words, all technologies are not the same, and someone with many years of technology experience in one area could be considered a novice in another.

It is worth mentioning here that *technology*, as used in this context, does not necessarily have to involve 1s and 0s, advanced physics, biology, or chemistry. The term should be thought to involve any type of specialized knowledge, such as a proprietary approach to process re-engineering, tax preparation, medicine, or architectural design, to name a few.

Technology impacts media selection in that whenever technology is the topic of communication you should consider your audience's familiarity with the specific technology under discussion. If your audience is experienced with the technology, then you might be safe using leaner media, but if the technology is new to them, then using richer communication is warranted. In this way, as questions arise about the specifics related to the technology, you will be able to clear up confusion before it takes root in your audience's mind.

StreetSmarts

While working in Silicon Valley, I used to sell advanced telecommunication networks to telecommunication managers. Quite often, my job was to sell our cutting-edge technology to major companies for beta sites. It would be natural to assume that an experienced telecommunication manager would understand the technology that I was selling, but that was often not the case. I would find that they would have major misconceptions about how the technology worked and how it would benefit them. If I had only sent an email or brochure, I would not have known about their confusion. The way I found out about it was from the feedback received in meetings - rich communication. Be careful not to fall into the trap of believing that experience in one technology area means understanding in another. When the technology discussion becomes non-routine, look to move to a richer form of communication.

Project Team Experience

If you have ever had the opportunity to work as a member of a highly functional team, you know that it is at the same time gratifying and a little spoiling. Once you have experienced an effective team, you know it can happen and continue to compare future teams to that experience. The good news is that those who understand highly functional teams are more likely to create them in the future. The unfortunate news is that teams rarely start out highly functional. They become highly functional as the result of a learning process that goes beyond skills and talent. The learning process involves the team members getting to know and trust each other, which involves experience.

Two people who have many experiences working with each other can create an understanding of how they interact such that one can anticipate the actions of the others. When one team member needs a tool, the other will have already picked up the tool, ready to hand it over when needed. There is almost a group thinking that happens with highly functional teams whereby they think and react as a group. Sometimes team thinking combines in a fluid way to address an ambiguous situation such that a creative answer to a question naturally evolves from the team member interaction. Everyone sees it as ambiguous, everyone adds their experience to the analysis and solution, and the experience used to "feel" the solution no longer represents that of an individual but the combined experience of the team. This is magical when it happens.

StreetSmarts

It may be fine to use lean media for much of the communication in a highly functioning team because much of their work may be routine to them all, given their common experiences. But beware of using lean media for an ambiguous situation that will be best addressed using the combined, interactive experiences of team members. Always use rich media for ambiguous situations.

Media selection is impacted by team experience should a new member join the team. At that point, this person is a novice to the team, and as such, team interactions should be considered non-routine. For the other team members to expect that person to be immediately highly functional is unrealistic, and richer media should be used in the early days to get her up to speed. She will quickly learn about the team, the team will learn about her, and the situation will eventually move toward more routine.

Customer Industry Experience

Just as we develop habits and expectations based on the culture within which we were raised, company personnel within specific industries develop expectations based on their experience within that particular industry. Consider a situation where a successful sales manager from a software development startup company has been hired to manage the sales of a startup construction products company. This manager has experience selling for a software startup company, but the two industries have radically different expectations and norms. The software world can release an application and, in a very short period of time, generate sales and make credible estimates about acceptance of the new product. The software application industry works on Internet time. New product decisions within the construction industry may take years to make and implement. It is not uncommon for large construction projects to be announced to bidders several years before the construction is to commence. In addition, the liabilities associated with product failure in the construction industry are so large, given the potential loss of life, that decisions in this industry are made at what our sales manager will likely view as a glacial pace. Should the sales projections of the new construction product be based on an expectation of Internet-time sales, feedback, and acceptance, there will surely be disappointments.

Again, here is a situation where substantial experience in one industry will not allow the manager to make seasoned decisions related to ambiguous situations based on the norms of a different industry. This person certainly understands sales, which is why she was hired, and she will eventually make a solid addition to the construction company's management team. However, it would make sense to ensure that seasoned people from within the construction industry are available as advisors to the new sales manager as she acclimates.

In other words, experience working in one industry does not translate to experience in another unrelated industry, which means communication with persons new to the industry should be treated as non-routine. Most likely, the new person will quickly learn the nuances of the new industry, but until that has happened, always ensure that periodic rich communication (mentoring) happens to ensure that your "new" person is understanding leaner messages as intended.

Media Matching Bottom Line Regarding Experience: The greater the experience level in any of these areas between the senders and the audience for a specific situation, the more you can lean toward a leaner form of communication for that area. If experience on either side in any of the key experience areas is lacking, then the situation should be treated as non-routine, which implies leaning toward richer communication media so that potential misunderstandings are more likely to be uncovered and addressed earlier. After an experience base has been developed, then it should be ok to move to leaner communications. Ambiguous situations should always be addressed with rich media.

Audience Receptivity

Recall that individuals have communication filters that shade their interpretation of received communications. People who like and trust you are more likely to interpret what you say in a positive light. People who do not like or trust you will often see negatives where none were intended. Anyone who has lived through an American presidential election year has seen this filtering phenomenon at work. The very same information mentioned by one candidate and interpreted by two news organizations with very different political outlooks (and agendas) will often have opposite interpretations of the information. Notice that the information did not change – only the interpretation of that information by the audience changed. Multiply this individual filtering effect by the number of people in your targeted audience group, and you get a sense of how difficult it is to create and deliver a message that will be received consistently by the audience group members.

A general rule of thumb is that friendly audiences will be more receptive to your message, and antagonistic audiences will be more likely to reject or misinterpret your message. I think this is an OK starting point, but it is too simplistic for a message of more than nominal complexity and where the outcome is important to you. Favorable audiences are likely to put a more favorable "spin" on what they hear, and antagonistic audiences are more likely to put a negative "spin" on what they hear. This means that both are highly prone to inaccurately hear the basic message because both will be inclined to filter out what they perceive as not applying to them (or do not like) and focus on what they perceive as important (what they like). Audiences tend to hear those things that justify their own beliefs, and research shows that people will seek out sources that promote viewpoints that the person already subscribes to. We tend to hear what will fulfill our expectations and complies with our beliefs. The danger is that you may believe your message was heard as intended when in reality, they understood their own version of things that may not resemble your intent at all. If their understanding and cooperation are important to you, then feedback is needed to confirm their understanding. Whenever you read "feedback," your mind should immediately jump to richer communication media, which is correct.

HOT TIP 🔥

There is a fascinating area of research going on that investigates the way that our minds make choices and evaluate risks. It turns out that our decision-making, and that of our audiences, is not as rational as we would like to believe, and this irrationality can cause us (them) to make choices in the moment that are not in our best interest. If you are interested in learning more about this topic, I suggest you check out *Thinking Fast and Slow*[9] by Daniel Kahneman. Kahneman was awarded the Nobel Prize in Economics for his work done with Amos Tversky. To learn more about the relationship between Kahneman and Tversky and how they developed their work, read *The Undoing Project*[10] by Michael Lewis. Interesting stuff.

Recall that cues and feedback allow for adapting your message and are a key consideration when determining the media richness level needed to deliver your message. For this reason, a town hall meeting venue is often used by political candidates to test new messages. A town hall is where the audience and presenter are in an informal venue where the candidate will deliver a message in person and receive instant feedback about how their message was received. Everyone hears the same words and is in the same room. The presenter can visually and personally gauge their reactions, and the audience members are typically encouraged to ask questions directly to the presenter. This level of feedback is simply not possible with broadcast television or radio, or newspaper delivery methods. Sure, television and radio are richer than the newspaper, BUT they are still broadcast media and, as such, provide little to no feedback to the candidate. The broadcast message could be improperly received, and the candidate would not find out until much later. For these reasons, candidates will often test a new message in a smaller venue format with facilitated face-to-face interaction. This approach allows the candidate to determine if the message was received as intended and refine the message content to make it more consistently understood. After the message is refined to an adequate level of confidence, it can be more reliably delivered using less rich broadcast media.

Movie production companies use a similar approach when determining scenes to keep in or remove from a movie. DVDs often contain a Deleted Scenes section which will contain alternate endings that were earlier presented to audiences, who then provided feedback as to the ending they most preferred. The most preferred ending was included in the general release version of the movie, and the lesser preferred were included as alternate DVD extra endings. Testing the movie on smaller audiences which provided quick feedback, increased the likelihood that the movie would be well received by the general viewing audience. Without the testing and feedback, the producers might find out that the ending was not well received by poor reviews and poor ticket sales, which would be much more difficult and expensive to overcome.

Media Matching Receptivity Bottom Line: If the audience is receptive to the sender's message, then a leaner media richness level should be fine. If the audience is more hostile in nature, then consider using a richer form of media to enable cue reading, feedback, and message clarification that may help overcome a misunderstanding due to the influence of antagonistic audience filters. If the situation is intensely emotional, consider using mediators who meet in person to represent the involved parties. This approach uses richer forms of communication while also offering one level of emotional separation. This is common practice in nasty divorce situations.

Culture: The Wild Card That Defines Environments

Just as the audience filters will influence the way that a message is received, audience culture can create an overall context within which all communication is interpreted. Culture is something that can override the best intentions on the part of the sender, and making a cultural mistake can eliminate all possibilities of productive follow-on communication.

One profound example I recall of culture-defining all else occurred while I was standing in a temple near Kyoto, Japan. Prominent signs in multiple languages near the visitor entrance to the temple clearly stated that shoes were not allowed in the temple. Bins were prominently provided where visitors could store their shoes while visiting. From my perspective, the quiet that came from not hearing the shoe heels clicking on the wooden floors added to the meditative state that many go there to experience, especially the local Japanese, for whom this might be a place of personal worship. While I was standing next to one of the temple guards, a woman refused to take off her shoes and walked directly into the temple. The guard politely moved to intercept her and motioned for her to take off her shoes. She waved him off and righteously walked directly into the temple, high heels clicking away. I was embarrassed for her and a little offended by her lack of consideration not only for the local customs but also for the other visitors, many of whom were not Japanese and had taken off their shoes.

In fairness, after I had visited half a dozen temples on the same day, I was tired of taking my shoes off, too, and could understand at some level how she might have felt. But I viewed myself as a visitor in their "house" and felt it only right to abide by their customs, a viewpoint that this woman obviously did not share. If her intended outcome was to induce goodwill toward her and other visitors, she blew it. If she wanted to show herself as a strong, independent woman, she blew that one too, in my opinion. If she wanted to demonstrate that she didn't care about the local customs, she was very successful. I can safely say that having seen the look on the face of the guard and the other visitors, if she had needed a ride to the train station, she would have had to walk, high heels and all.

Cultural norms do not have to be as obvious as the prior Japanese example. They might be as simple as punctuality. Assume that you are looking to cultivate a healthy, productive business alliance with another company. Assume that both sides agreed to meet at 2:00 PM, and they show up at 2:30 PM without making any effort to let you know about their tardiness. Assume also that you had both arranged for your top management to attend the meeting, due to its importance, and they show up with a single lower-level member of their staff. If your organization has a culture where punctuality is valued, then this relationship has definitely gotten off on the wrong foot. Your management would have much justification for wondering if the other side would treat its future commitments as casually as they did the starting time for this initial meeting. They might also wonder about your effectiveness in that you arranged for your executive team to attend when the other side had no intentions of doing the same. Their meeting mistake could jeopardize the future potential relationship between the two companies and possibly tarnish your career.

Think of organizational culture as a wild card in that it is difficult to overcome a strongly entrenched cultural perception. Not being sensitive to the cultural perceptions of the audience is asking for an invisible disappointment. I say invisible in that it is the rare customer who is going to tell you that something you did or said offended the audience members to the point that they are no longer interested in continuing communication. More likely, they will simply not respond to future communication requests or be glacially polite while allowing no progress with relationship development. There is no need on their part. They have already determined that you are not someone with whom they want to do business.

Media Matching Cultural Bottom Line: Culture may define how you need to communicate. If there is a large cross-cultural divide, then lean toward using a richer form of media. If you, as the presenter, share the same culture as the audience, then from a cultural standpoint, you could be OK using a leaner form of media. That said, if the audience culture is one that always uses email and seriously frowns on face-to-face, then you will likely have to figure out a way to use email in the richest possible way should the situation be non-routine. Trying to force a face-to-face meeting will likely work against you in the context of this example. On the other hand, if you sincerely believe that the relationship will be lost without the meeting, you have little to lose by pushing for the face-to-face meeting. This is a sensitive area, and seeking guidance from your audience is a great idea, if possible. Quite often, they will gladly clue you in on their cultural norms if just asked.

Risk: Another Wild Card That Dictates Everything

People don't often consider *risk* when selecting a media, which is a mistake. We all have been successful at managing risks in the past, or candidly we would not be here. Risk is an integral part of daily personal and business life, and developing a sensitivity to risk assessment on the part of your audience is critical to communication success. When someone perceives a situation as risky, they will likely avoid it if possible, and any related subsequent communication will be viewed as dubious because it will be filtered through a risky lens. To understand and manage risk, it is important to break the risk analysis we intuitively perform into its component parts. The communication value of this approach is to help you understand risk from their perspective, which enables you to help your audience walk through the risk assessment logically instead of simply making an intuitive choice that may be more based on emotion than fact. Understanding the "risks of failure" inherent in a situation provides you with advanced insight that allows you to take the actions needed to decrease the negative risk perception.

Risk analysis involves several components. First, something of value must be at risk, which is something tangible like money, property, time, or health, or something intangible like reputation or career advancement. Second, some type of event(s) must be perceived as possibly happening that could jeopardize what we have at risk. Third, what is the percentage likelihood that these events may occur? A high percentage likelihood means that it is highly likely to occur, and a low percentage likelihood means the opposite. Fourth, what is the perceived impact on the organization or person should the events occur? Fifth, what is the personal or organizational risk tolerance to withstanding the perceived impact? A higher risk tolerance means that the organization or person can withstand the impact with minimal jeopardy, and a low-risk tolerance means that the organization could be seriously damaged by the risk impact.

Thinking back to our earlier discussion about uncertainty and ambiguity, risk can be thought of as an emotionally uncertain situation in the mind of your audience. Your audience may perceive something as risky when, in reality, the risk is small. If you can uncover their perceived risks and then provide information that shows those risks to be minimal, you may be able to move a highly risky situation into one perceived as manageable. The risk detailing process will be most productively accomplished using rich media, and you may then be able to move to leaner media to offer the pertinent information. Make sure to confirm their understanding along the way, always being aware that risk and survival are the lenses through which your messages will be interpreted.

StreetSmarts

In fairness, your audience's perception of something being of high risk might be correct. This process, when done objectively, will uncover that as well. Should this happen, then you and your audience will now understand things the same way, which means that complete communication has happened. From that point, a constructive conversation can be had about ways of mitigating the risks, which may still present an opportunity for both you and them.

Think of risk as another wild card in that if the audience perceives something as high risk to them, then they are going to want to use rich media to get as many cues and as much feedback as possible in assessing the risk and uncertainty for themselves. As the sender, if you think that the audience could perceive the communication or situation as high risk, then you want to use the richest possible media available. In a risky situation, folks will interpret things more negatively than when the risk is normal, and the likelihood of misunderstanding is high due to heightened risk filtering. With rich media, you are more likely to see this shift in the audience and address the perception before it becomes so deeply entrenched in the audience's thinking that it becomes very difficult to shift.

Here is an example of how we naturally want to escalate media when we perceive a situation as risky. Assume that you have a family member who has just been involved in a major car accident and is in the hospital's critical care ward. Assume also that when you ask about your loved one's condition, the receptionist gives you a sheet of paper with a message from the doctor that describes the symptoms and offers a prognosis. If you are like most people I know, your response would be something like, "Huh?! What am I supposed to do with this? When can I talk to the doctor in charge?" The risk for you is so high that you want to hear it directly from the doctor so you can make your own assessment of the situation. You may not have the expertise of a doctor, but you can read the doctor who has the expertise while she relays the details of your loved one's situation. No piece of paper can fill that feedback/ cue need prompted by the high perceived risk level because the paper is just not a rich enough media. If you are the sender of a message for which you have a personal risk, then you might also want to use richer media to ensure that your message is properly received. Again, an email might provide the information, but the face-to-face meeting will offer you the cues and feedback that will enable you to confirm that your message was received as intended. There is no guarantee that they will act in the way you want, but by ensuring that your "risky" message gets past the filters to be received as intended, you have eliminated one area of possible trouble in achieving your outcome.

Media Matching Bottom Line About Risk: Evaluate the Perceived Risk from both the perspective of the sender and receiver. If the Perceived Risk level is high on either side of the communication, then tend toward a richer form of communication. Make this determination independent of how the other audience and situational factors would influence the media selection process. As the risk begins to be perceived as manageable, it may be safe to tend toward leaner communication but never lose awareness that the risk filters were once in play.

Chapter Summary

It is difficult to overemphasize the importance of the audience in any communication. The typical communicator tends to think that as the sender, his side of the communication is of paramount importance when, in reality, the audience holds the cooperation cards. It just makes sense to consider the audience as an integral aspect of any communication designed to achieve a desired outcome. This chapter presented a framework within which you can assess key audience characteristics in such a way that enables informed message development and complementary media selection for the delivery of that message.

It is important to take the time to assess the experience level of the audience in at least the areas presented, their receptivity to you and your message, the cultural filters through which the message will be interpreted, and the perceived risk that audience members will attach to the message. At first, this may seem like a lot to consider, but it will quickly become second nature. Before entering an important communication situation, take a few moments to apply the concepts presented. If you realize that something is unknown in one of these areas, especially in the risk and culture areas, then take the time to learn more about the audience. This will increase your odds of ensuring that the right message is delivered to the right audience using the right method of communication. What they do with the message once received is up to them. Taking this approach will better ensure that your message is received as intended, which goes a long way toward fostering communication and, ultimately, cooperation.

Paulson Media Matching Method Overview

The goal of any communication is for the receiver to understand a message as the message sender intended. At this point, it should be clear that any chance of complete and effective communication starts with careful consideration of the audience and your communication goals. In the prior chapters, we covered many topics such as routineness, complexity, experience, and risk and explained their importance in selecting the media richness level that best ensures message understanding. It is a lot to consider, and it would make sense to create a simple way for applying the various concepts so that you can quickly size up the situation and select the proper richness level. That is the point of this chapter: to introduce you to the Paulson Media Matching Method, which is a chart that helps you easily structure what you know about your audience and the situation, which you then use to select the best media richness level for message delivery. After a short time, you will automatically be able to size up a situation and determine the proper media, but at first, you will likely find the chart helpful. Remember also that using the chart protects you from missing something when planning your communications.

Effective communication involves a blend of critical thinking, an awareness of those around you, and a realistic assessment of possible options from which you can develop the best message that will gain audience cooperation. This topic is so important that the entirety of book 2 in this book series, "Getting Agreement: Designing Messages that Create Cooperation," is dedicated to message development. Communication designers must always understand that the most excellent plan of action can meet with hazardous results if it is misinterpreted by the stakeholders who must implement it. Media selection is critical to ensuring the most accurate message receipt and interpretation, which is the point of the Paulson Media Matching Method.

THE PAULSON MEDIA MATCHING METHOD

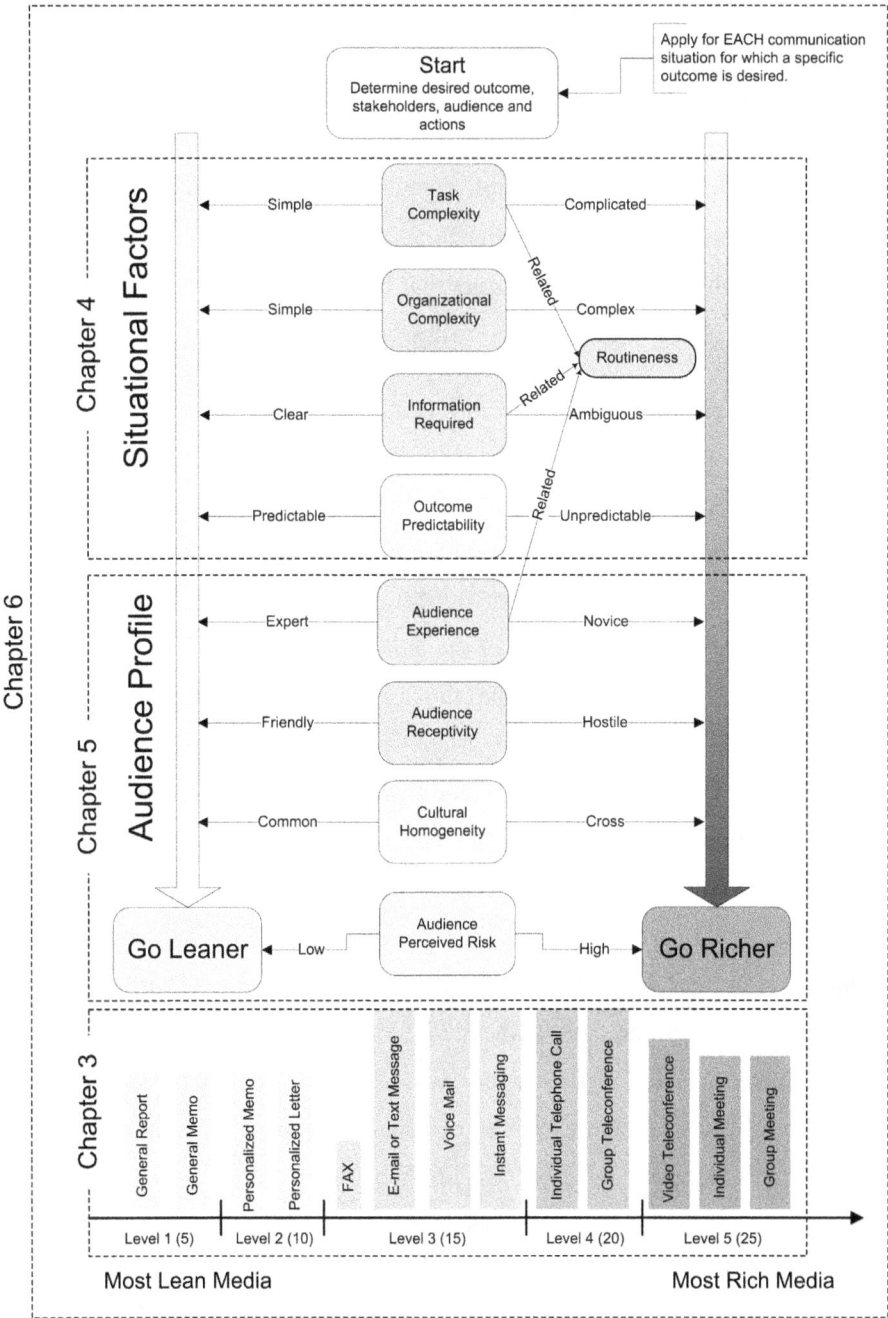

Start
Determine desired outcome, stakeholders, audience and actions

Apply for EACH communication situation for which a specific outcome is desired.

Chapter 4 — Situational Factors

Simple	Task Complexity	Complicated
Simple	Organizational Complexity	Complex
		Routineness
Clear	Information Required	Ambiguous
Predictable	Outcome Predictability	Unpredictable

Related

Chapter 5 — Audience Profile

Expert	Audience Experience	Novice
Friendly	Audience Receptivity	Hostile
Common	Cultural Homogeneity	Cross

Go Leaner ◄ Low — Audience Perceived Risk — High ► **Go Richer**

Chapter 3

General Report
General Memo
Personalized Memo
Personalized Letter
FAX
E-mail or Text Message
Voice Mail
Instant Messaging
Individual Telephone Call
Group Teleconference
Video Teleconference
Individual Meeting
Group Meeting

Level 1 (5)	Level 2 (10)	Level 3 (15)	Level 4 (20)	Level 5 (25)

Most Lean Media   Most Rich Media

Chapter 6

Explaining the Paulson Media Matching Method

Chapters 3, 4, and 5 presented many concepts related to media richness, evaluating the situation within which communication occurs and assessing the audience. The Paulson Media Matching Method chapter ties these concepts together to provide a simple framework within which you can select the most appropriate media for a given message, situation, audience, and intended outcome. Notice in the figure that there are areas surrounded by dashed lines that highlight the relationship to earlier chapters.

At the bottom of the figure are the various media richness levels presented in Chapter 3, with the leanest media on the left side (General Report) and increasing to the richest on the right (Interactive Group Meeting). The blocks listed vertically in the center of the page correspond to the concepts presented in the chapters related to your Situation (Chapter 4) and Audience (Chapter 5) evaluations. For each of the individual concepts, there is an ideal "lean" or "rich" media selection, and the designation for each is listed on the arrows pointing either left or right. For example, the "Task Complexity" block shows "Simple" tasks should tend toward using "Leaner" media, whereas "Complicated" tasks should tend toward "Richer" media. The same "tendencies" are listed for the other blocks. Notice that "Outcome Predictability" is a different shade from the other situational factors and that "Cultural Homogeneity" and "Audience Perceived Risk Level" are also a different shade from the other audience factors. This is because they fall into the special "Wild Card" category, where their characteristics do not just contribute to determining the overall best media richness for a situation but can dictate the proper media richness on their own. Topics covered in a given chapter are enclosed in a box with the appropriate chapter number noted.

Remember that a key intent of this model is to enable you, as the message sender, to proactively determine the delivery media that best ensures that your message is received as intended. On the surface, picking the right media seems like it should be a simple thing to accomplish, but as we have discussed throughout the book and as we have all experienced in our own lives, proper media matching is far more complicated than it first appears. All of the listed situational, audience, and richness influences must be considered to put the likelihood of being properly understood on your side. The Paulson Media Matching Method is your systematic approach to being understood. Use it to ensure that your message gets through as intended.

Using the Paulson Media Matching Method Chart

Assume that you are presented with a situation where the cooperation of another person is needed to achieve your intended outcome. Assume that you have a good working relationship with this person. You know your intended outcome and now must take steps that move your audience in the direction of helping you to achieve your outcome. Assume that the message you want to be understood is a specific audience action. Let's apply the Paulson Media Matching Method to see how the right media would be selected.

First, let's look at the "Situational Factors." Assume that the action you are requesting from the receiver is nothing out of the ordinary for you or them, making the task "Simple" in complexity, which implies that you can tend toward a leaner communication media selection. Assume that there are no extraordinary political or personal complications involved with the situation, which again is "Simple" and implies again that you can tend toward leaner media richness. Assume that the level of involved information is "Clear" and that your expectation that the receiver will be able to successfully complete the requested action is high ("Predictable"), which also tends toward a leaner form of communication.

Now let's look at the "Audience Profile" considerations. Notice from the first line of the preceding paragraph that you have had a good prior working relationship with the receiver, making Audience Receptivity "Friendly," which points toward the use of leaner media. Assuming that there are no Cultural Homogeneity issues ("Common") or Audience Perceived Risk issues present ("Low") to override the assessment, then this is the type of situation where a leaner form of communication has a high likelihood of achieving your desired outcome. This message could be sent by e-mail (Level 3). You could choose to send a letter or paper memo, but in today's work environment, a memo would be unlikely and inefficient. The key point of this example is that you now have, in advance, determined the proper media and tool (email) to use to deliver a routine message to an experienced, friendly audience.

Let's add a little spice to the situation. Assume that all the prior factors are still accurate with one additional influence: Upper management has specifically asked you and the receiver to never again do exactly what you are requesting. Notice how all the factors presented previously still indicate that email or lower would be the right richness level, but adding the upper management edict raised the Perceived Risk to you and the receiver to "High." As soon as the perceived risk escalates for either of you, then tend toward a richer form of communication which would be either telephone (Level 4) or, if very risky, a face-to-face meeting (Level 5). Can you now see how risk acts as an override?

Let's play with this same situation a little more by removing the upper management risk factor introduced in the last paragraph and modifying the experience and routineness influences. Assume that the receiver is new to the company, new to you, and has never been asked to perform this particular set of tasks before. Notice how Audience Experience moved to "Novice," and the Task Complexity for this novice may now be more "Complicated," which moves the situation from Routine to Non-Routine. Where previously an email would have worked well, you would now tend towards using richer media. Also, consider that if this person is somewhat concerned about perceptions, being new to the company and all, they might also perceive the "Risk" level as "high" associated with the request, which also tends toward richer media selection. If the needed actions are mission-critical to you (high risk), then you would most definitely want to err on the side of richer communication. In this case, you would probably tend toward using the telephone (Level 4) or a face-to-face (Level 5) meeting.

A key concept from this set of examples is that the same requested actions may be construed in very different ways based on the specific situational and audience influences involved. Simply thinking that this request is trivial because these actions were common to you or your receiver's predecessor does not consider the reality of a very important part in achieving your desired outcome: this particular receiver.

Interpreting "Tendency Toward"

We have talked about each of the influences as adding a "tendency" toward using a certain level of richness over another, and the tendency is really the right way to think about the influences other than the wild card influences. For example, when multiple influences align toward the same very lean or very rich, media selection is simple to evaluate. For example, if the influences are "Complicated," "Complex," "Ambiguous," and "Novice," you would certainly tend toward a Level 4 or Level 5 richness level. On the other hand, if the influences are "Simple," "Clear," and "Expert," then you would certainly tend toward using a leaner richness level such as a report or email. But what happens when the influences are not so clearly defined? That is where the tendencies come into play. If all influences are average but the "Organizational Complexity" assessment is "Complex," then you would probably want to make a telephone call to the receiver to clear up any misunderstandings that might come up if only email had been used. If nothing else, use the phone call to explain what you plan to put into the email to help avoid misunderstandings. Your previous experience with the person, in conjunction with the routineness of the situation, would offset the extreme complexity and not necessarily require a Level 5 media. On the other hand, if there was no prior experience when dealing with a non-routine and complex situation, you should try to use Level 5, face-to-face meeting media, if possible.

A Numeric Approach to the Required Richness Assessment Chart

As you become more familiar with applying the Paulson Media Matching Method, it will quickly become intuitive and second nature. You will eventually perform the assessment without really thinking about it and naturally find yourself intuitively selecting the proper media from the available options. You will start to recognize situations where others chose a mismatched message and/or media richness only to watch problems arise that could have been avoided simply by matching the right media and message for that specific situation and audience.

StreetSmarts

No communication method can anticipate all possible situations or influences, and all methods are only as effective as the people applying them. Never forget that your mind is the most powerful situational assessment tool in existence, and you should use the chart to structure your thinking and to ensure nothing is overlooked.

A "Numeric Richness Assessment Chart" is offered as a learning tool that you can use while developing your media richness intuition. Again, I want to emphasize that these charts are most useful when used as tendency indicators and not as absolute rules that must be followed.

Here is how you can use the Richness Chart. Notice the "Richness Needed" block in the middle of the figure. This block has a numeric spread from 5

NUMERIC RICHNESS ASSESSMENT CHART

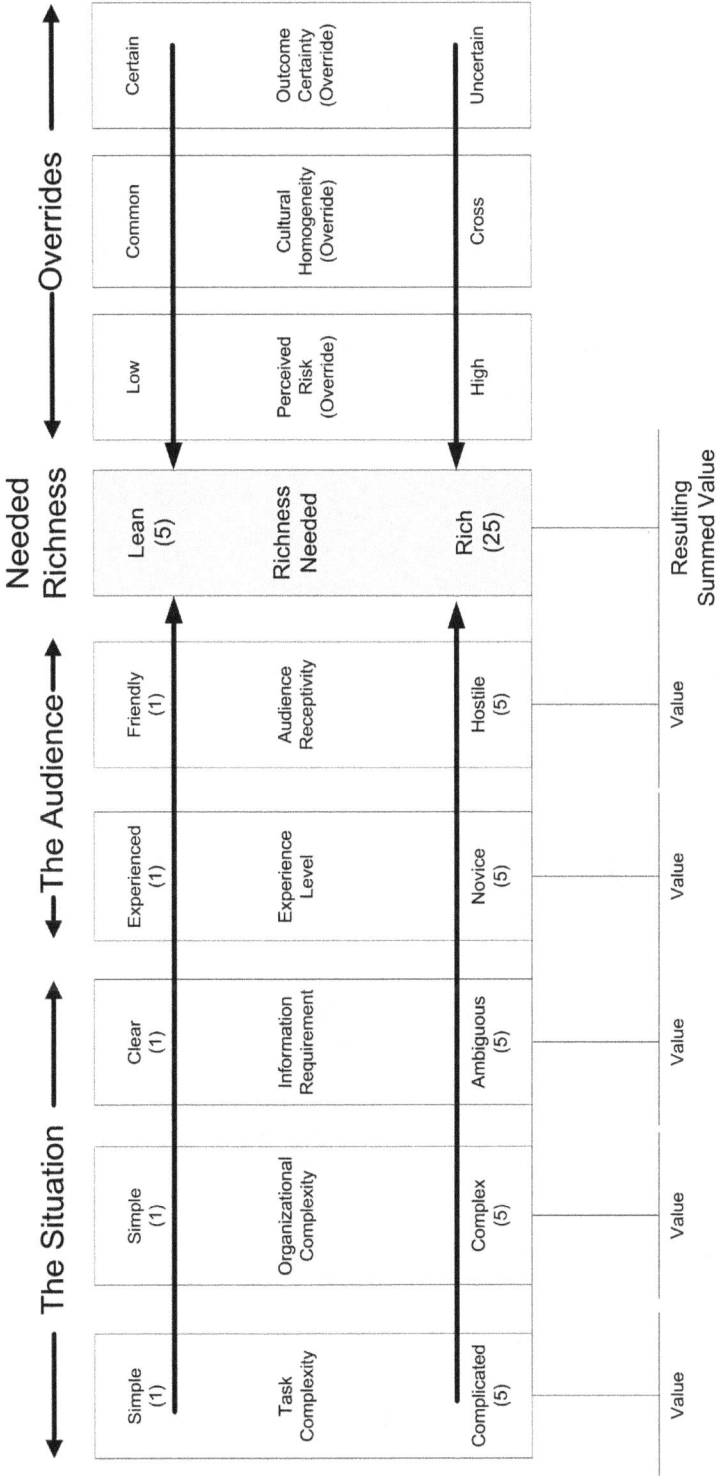

The Situation				The Audience		Needed Richness	Overrides		
Simple (1)	Simple (1)	Clear (1)	Experienced (1)	Friendly (1)		Lean (5)	Low	Common	Certain
Task Complexity	Organizational Complexity	Information Requirement	Experience Level	Audience Receptivity		Richness Needed	Perceived Risk (Override)	Cultural Homogeneity (Override)	Outcome Certainty (Override)
Complicated (5)	Complex (5)	Ambiguous (5)	Novice (5)	Hostile (5)		Rich (25)	High	Cross	Uncertain
Value	Value	Value	Value	Value		Resulting Summed Value			

(lean) to 25 (rich). The blocks to the left of "Richness Needed" represent each of the situational and audience influences, with the lean extreme given a value of "1" and the rich extreme given a value of "5." If all of the Situation and Audience influences tended toward lean then the sum of the blocks would equal 1+1+1+1+1=5, corresponding to "Lean" on the "Richness" block. Conversely, if each influence tended toward rich, then the sum of the blocks would equal 5+5+5+5+5=25, corresponding to the "Rich" designation. To the right are the wild card influences (Overrides) with their respective lean and rich media indicators. The numeric "Richness Needed" values calculated on the second figure are related to the richness levels shown on the Paulson Media Matching figure shown as the number in brackets on the bottom row. Again, if any of the Overrides indicate the use of richer media, then that should be given strong consideration.

Caution ⚠

Don't try to apply the Paulson Media Matching Method to a communication situation without having read the explanations offered in the previous chapters. There is a high likelihood that your interpretation of the various factors will not match those of the method. For example, you may think that you understand what is meant by "Routineness," but after many years of working with people applying this method, I can tell you that folks rarely interpret it in the way meant for use with the media matching method. It is critical to understand the blended nature of task complexity, information complexity, and experience before you can accurately make a routineness determination.

Chapter Summary

The prior chapters introduced important concepts that contribute to determining the level of media richness you should use for a particular communication situation. These concepts were tied together in this chapter with the Paulson Media Matching Method. Correctly performing this simple analysis in advance of communicating will enable you to determine the best media to use for delivering your message to best ensure that your audience will understand it as you intended. Book Two in this book series, "Getting Agreement: Designing Messages that Create Cooperation," offers a systematic approach for developing the message that you ultimately want your audience to understand and is a great companion to this book.

As a media-matching learning tool, a numerical approach to determining richness was included to help you develop a nuanced feel for its application. After a short period of time, you will find yourself intuitively applying the concepts and determining the proper richness level. Combining all of this will make you more likely to receive audience cooperation, and your communication successes will make it easier to work with others.

A final comment is warranted about the potential for using the media matching method as a diagnostic tool. Should you find yourself in a situation where you followed the method but were misunderstood, look at the method and evaluate your assumptions related to the various components. You might find that you missed something the first time that, if corrected, would give you a chance to correct your earlier miscommunication and get things back on track. Or it might be the message itself, in which case you can apply the method in "Getting Agreement" in a similar diagnostic way.

Conclusion And Preview Of The Outcome Oriented Communication Method

There is a lot involved with becoming an effective business communicator. Effective, in this case, means becoming a communicator who has a high likelihood of achieving your desired communication goals. Contrary to what most people think, we are not all born effective communicators, and usually, only through painful learning and experience do we become more effective.

You should now see that the only way to make clear communication happen is through planning. You must design your communication approach around your audience. You must craft a message that will motivate your audience to act as you intend and then use delivery media correctly to ensure it is understood. Combining all of this smoothly requires forethought and practice. It requires planning. It requires a method to ensure that key ingredients are not overlooked. The prior chapters detailed the delivery media matching method, and Book Two, "Getting Agreement," gives you an approach to message development.

We have repeatedly discussed the value of proactively using communication analysis when looking to achieve a communication outcome. We saw in Chapters 3 to 5 that using a communication media with improperly matched richness for a given situation can create misunderstanding problems where none previously existed. Considering the various influences IN ADVANCE of initiating a communication allows the message sender to better ensure that the message will be received as intended. Otherwise, a great message sent using the wrong media could require the sender to spend valuable time correcting misperceptions that could have been avoided had the influences been considered and the proper media richness selected. This is an essential premise of proactive communication: think and plan the communication that is most likely to get you your intended outcome BEFORE initiating the communication. If you know where you want to go and have taken the needed preparation steps to get there, you are simply more likely to get where you want to go, bringing the audience along with you.

We saw that business communication is typically goal focused and almost always driven by the need to accomplish something as efficiently as possible. We also saw that organizations function through the actions of individuals and groups and that without their cooperation, little gets done. As a result, it is critical to always focus communication on the intended audience and stakeholders instead of on yourself and your presentation skills. Sure, your presentation skills are important, but great skills that do not consider the needs and characteristics of your intended audience won't help you become a great communicator and get the results you desire.

We dug deeply into the important and often neglected role of feedback in communication design and looked at how different media have a richness level that makes them more appropriate for one communication situation over another. You should now have a deeper appreciation for the role of experience in determining media selection, as well as the importance of situation and task complexity as you select your media. Tied in with this are the important override considerations of culture and risk, which are often completely ignored by communicators but can derail any chance of success before it gets started.

There is an important value derived from using a structured method for addressing a communication situation. I have found that it is always better to ponder as many aspects of an important communication situation as possible before communicating with my intended audience. This keeps me from making major errors that could have been avoided had I just thought about it a little more in advance.

Caution ⚠

It is always easier to not say something that is unnecessary than to say something that is interpreted incorrectly and negatively interpreted by the audience.

Err on the side of planning, analysis, and caution before communicating, and then deliver your message with skill and sincerity, and you will find people to be more willing partners in your journey. You want to achieve your business goals, and so does your audience. We all want to be successful, and we need each other to make that happen. It is also human nature to want to be understood. Audiences have a vested interest in completely understanding your communications just as much as you want to be understood. The more we all take the time to consider the best way to communicate something to others, the more receptive we all will be to each other and the more willing we will be to cooperate to everyone's benefit.

Book Two in this book series, "Getting Agreement: Designing Messages that Created Cooperation," offers a systematic approach to developing the right message for the right audience based on the organizational circumstances and desired outcomes. Book Three in the series "Flexibly Tough: Building Resilient Organizations Using Communication" offers a manager's framework for matching workers to tasks and then supporting them with a communication framework that improves their likelihood of successfully completing those tasks. Adopting the approach in "Flexibly Tough" will keep managers from being caught off guard by an employee-task mismatch that jeopardizes project and organizational success. Later books will present the application of these communication concepts in specific environments such as sales, marketing, and customer service, as well as project management. The overall goal of the entire series is for you and your personnel to become familiar with the Outcome Oriented Communication Method (see the following figure), which will make you the best, most successful communicators possible, creating cooperation and a sense of accomplishment, not only for you but also for those in your orbit. Thank you for coming along.

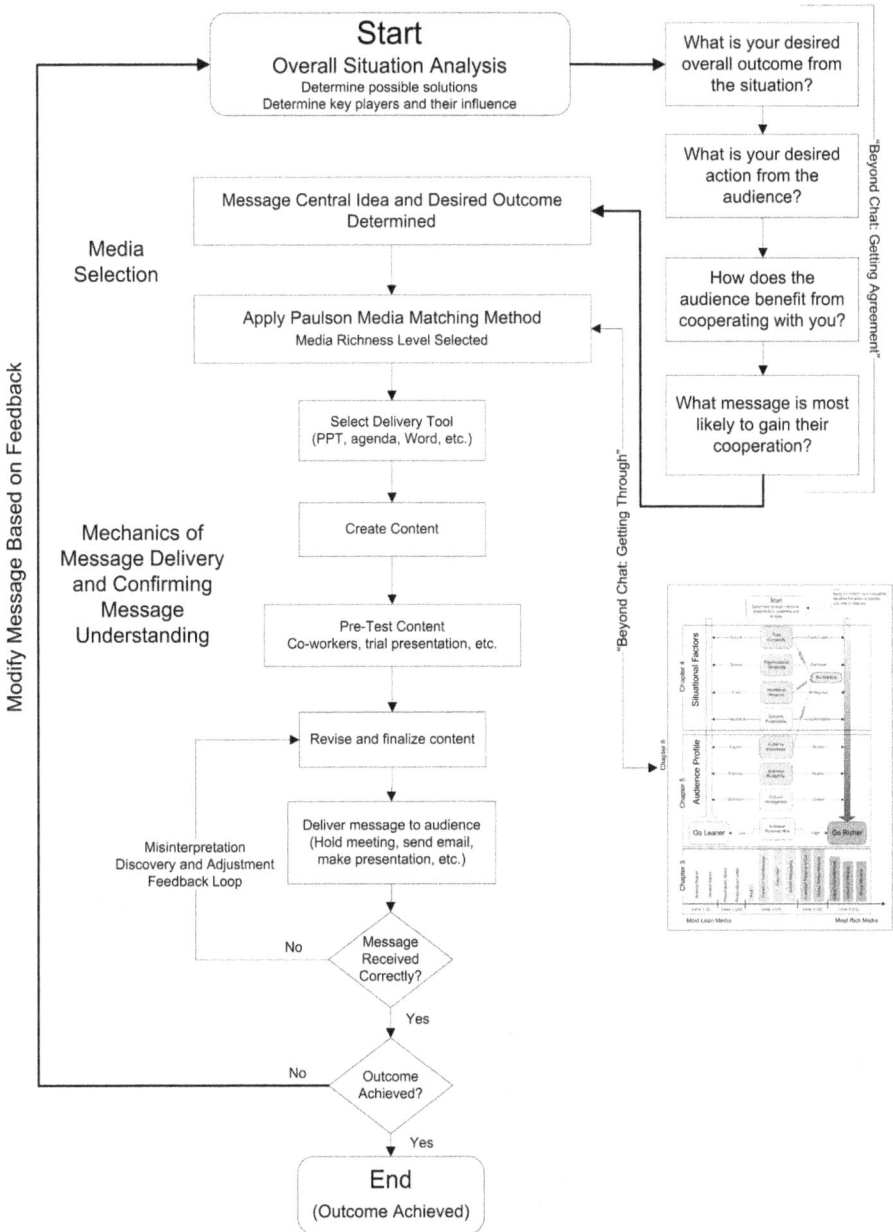

GENERALIZED OUTCOME ORIENTED COMMUNICATION METHOD

Start
Overall Situation Analysis
Determine possible solutions
Determine key players and their influence

What is your desired overall outcome from the situation?

What is your desired action from the audience?

Message Central Idea and Desired Outcome Determined

How does the audience benefit from cooperating with you?

Media Selection

Apply Paulson Media Matching Method
Media Richness Level Selected

What message is most likely to gain their cooperation?

Select Delivery Tool
(PPT, agenda, Word, etc.)

Create Content

Mechanics of Message Delivery and Confirming Message Understanding

Pre-Test Content
Co-workers, trial presentation, etc.

Revise and finalize content

Misinterpretation Discovery and Adjustment Feedback Loop

Deliver message to audience
(Hold meeting, send email, make presentation, etc.)

No → Message Received Correctly?

Yes

No → Outcome Achieved?

Yes

End
(Outcome Achieved)

Modify Message Based on Feedback

"Beyond Chat: Getting Agreement"

"Beyond Chat: Getting Through"

References

Chapter Two:

1. Frederick Herzberg, *The Motivation to Work*. (New York, NY: Wiley, 1959).

2. Anonymous, *Principles of Management*. (University of Minnesota Open-Source Library, 2022) Chapter 12.4: Communication Barriers. URL: https://open.lib.umn.edu/principlesmanagement/chapter/12-4-communi-cation-barriers/#:~:text=Barriers%20to%20Effective%20Communica-tion&text=These%20include%20filtering%2C%20selective%20percep-tion,and%20Receiver%2C%20and%20biased%20language.

3. Pantone.com. *About Pantone* (2022) URL: https://www.pantone.com/about-pantone#:~:text=About%20Pantone%20Standards,color%20any-where%20in%20the%20world.

4. Richard Daft, Robert Lengel, *Information Richness: A New Approach to Managerial Behavior and Organizational Design*. (Greenwich CT: JAI Press, 1984)

Chapter Three:

1. Richard Daft, Robert Lengel, *Information Richness: A New Approach to Managerial Behavior and Organizational Design*. (Greenwich CT: JAI Press, 1984)

2. Ronald Rice "Task Analyzability, Use of New Media and Effectiveness: A multi-Site Exploration of Media Richness," *Organizational Science* Vol 3, No. 4 (1992) pp. 475-500.

Chapter Four:

1. Perrow, C. (1967) "A Framework for the Comparative Analysis of Organizations," *American Psychological Review* Vol. 32, No. 2 (1967) pp. 194-208.

2. Richard Daft, Robert Lengel, *Information Richness: A New Approach to Managerial Behavior and Organizational Design.* (Greenwich CT: JAI Press, 1984)

3. Jay Galbraith, "Organization Design: An Information Processing View," *Interfaces* Vol. 4, No. 3, (1974) pp. 28-36.

4. SEC.gov (2010: Deepwater Horizon Accident Investigation Report. URL: https://www.sec.gov/Archives/edgar/data/313807/000119312510216268/dex993.htm#:~:text=The%20accident%20on%20April%2020,and%20subsequent%20ignition%20of%20hydrocarbons.

5. Daniel Kahneman, *Thinking, Fast and Slow.* (New York: Farrar, Strauss and Giroux, 2011).

Chapter Five:

1. Daniel Morrow, Von Leirer, Patsy Altieri, "Aging, Expertise and Narrative Processing," *Psychology and Aging* Vol. 7, No. 3, (1992) pp. 376-388.

2. Ker-Wei Pei, Hal Reneau, "The Effects of Memory Structure on Using Rule-Based Expert Systems for Training: A Framework and an Empirical Test," *Decision Science* Vol. 21, No. 2, (1990) p. 263

3. Dean Buonomano, *Brain Bugs: How the brain's flaws shape our lives.* (New York, NY: W.W. Norton & Company, 2011).

4. Carol Kuhlthau, "The role of experience in the information search process of an early career information worker: Perceptions of uncertainty, com-

plexity, construction, and sources," *Journal of the American Society for Information Science* Vol 50, No. 5 (1999) p. 399

5. Jose Esteves, Roy Chan, Joan Pastor, Michale Rosemann, "An Exploratory Study of Knowledge Types Relevance Along Enterprise Systems Implementation Phases," *4th European Conference on Organizational Knowledge and Learning Capabilities* (2003, April) Barcelona, Spain.

6. Blaize Reich, "Managing Knowledge and Learning in IT Projects: A Conceptual Framework and Guidelines for Practice," *Project Management Journal,* Vol. 38, No. 2 (2007)

7. Dan Remenyi, *Stop IT Project Failure through Risk Management.* (Oxford, England: Butterworth-Heinemann, 1999)

8. David Finnegan, Leslie Willcocks, "Knowledge Sharing Issues in the Introduction of New Technology," *Journal of Enterprise Information Management* Vol. 19, No. 6 (2006)

9. Daniel Kahneman, *Thinking, Fast and Slow.* (New York, NY: Farrar, Strauss and Giroux, 2011).

10. Michael Lewis, *The Undoing Project.* (New York, NY: WW Norton & Company, 2016).

11. John Anderson, Ram Narasimhan, "Assessing Project Implementation Risk: A Methodological Approach," *Management Science* Vol. 25, No. 6 (1979) Pp. 512-521.

Glossary

Ambiguity: A situation where experts viewing the same information will come to different opinions, and no additional information can be provided to enhance understanding. Actions taken to address ambiguous situations are usually decided based on the character of the persons making the final decision.

Audience: The intended recipient of your message from whom you will typically want some level of cooperation and subsequent action. (See Receiver too.)

Broadcast Media: A method of message delivery that offers limited opportunity for feedback and that feedback is typically very slow, not allowing for timely message adjustment.

Communication Channel: The technology conduit through which the message travels, such as cable, Wi-Fi, cellular or other technologies. (Also see Communication Link.)

Communication Link: The physical medium over which a message is sent, such as air for in-person communication, print or digital for a newspaper, or electromagnetic for radio. (Also see Communication Channel.)

Confirmation: The third step in the Complete Communication Model is whereby the sender confirms to the audience that their understanding of the sent message was accurate and/or where their understanding is incorrect.

Critical Thinking: The process of evaluating information from various viewpoints to determine a course of action. This typically involves some type of information search and analysis process which will be done using some type of communication.

Data: A measurement of some kind.

Equivocal: Another way of referring to a highly non-routine situation that is complicated and still assumed solvable with available information. An expert will determine the needed information that will typically be applied in a unique way. This is one step short of becoming ambiguous.

Experience: The aggregate knowledge gained by a person from having previously performed some action. There are diverse areas of experience, and experience in one area does not necessarily translate into experience in another.

Expert: A person who has extensive knowledge about a situation typically obtained through a combination of education and experience. Experts are capable of advanced critical thinking.

Feedback: A process by which the sender of a message can determine how accurately their sent message was received and interpreted by the Audience. This is the second step in the Complete Communication Model.

Information: What is obtained from comparing multiple pieces of data to each other.

Intuition: A subconscious process whereby the mind analyzes a situation through a lens of experience, education, skill, and knowledge to arrive at a conclusion, usually before the conscious mind is aware.

Knowledge: The process by which a person attaches meaning to the information obtained from comparing data. The ability to develop this meaning is derived from typically achieved through experience and/or education.

Media Richness: The speed and ability of a message delivery process to deliver information between sender and receiver such that understanding between sender and receiver can be enhanced.

Message: The ultimate concept(s) that the sender of a message wants to communicate to the message receiver.

Non-Routine: A situation where a high level of critical thinking is required to achieve a desired outcome.

Novice: A person with limited education, experience, or knowledge with respect to the situation.

Outcome: The desired result from a specific communication situation.

Outcome Uncertainty: A personal assessment of the likelihood that the sender will achieve her desired communication outcome.

Primary audience: The person(s) who will be the initial recipient of the delivered message and who is often the primary stakeholder as well.

Project: A special activity that is usually outside the realm of typical activities that has a specific start and start date and intended outcome.

Project Manager: A person responsible for coordinating the activities of various groups of people to achieve a special outcome.

Receiver: The person or group of people to whom a message is sent. (See Audience too.)

Responsibility without authority: A situation where a person or group of people are responsible for the outcome (success) of a given situation and have little to no direct control over the persons who will do the work to achieve the outcome.

Richness: A measurement of the ability of a media to deliver information such that understanding between the sender and receiver can be enhanced. Varies from Lean (low richness) to Rich (high richness).

Risk: The perception in the mind of a person that is related to something of theirs that has value and the likelihood that it can be lost.

Routineness: A measure of the complexity of a task as well as the perceived complexity of the task in the mind of the person who will complete the task. Routineness is a blend of task characteristics and the experience level of the responsible person.

Routine Situation: A situation where any exceptions can be dealt with through an established referral process to information and knowledge that already exists. These situations typically require simple critical thinking processes and are best assigned to novice persons.

Secondary Audience: A person or group of people who may be involved in a situation but are not part of the initial communications. These could also be secondary stakeholders.

Sender: The person developing and sending a message to others with the intention of creating some type of understanding that typically, in business, leads to receiver action or outcome.

Skill: The practical application of knowledge.

Stakeholder: Any person or group of people who are in some way affected by a given situation. This may be a direct stakeholder as well as a secondary stakeholder.

Technology: The application of scientific principles for practical use. Technology in this context is more than something operating with 1 and 0 and can include biological, chemical, engineering, architectural, and other fields. The manual printing press, at one point in time, was considered advanced technology.

Tool: The specific communication approach used for a given communication process. Typical tools include PowerPoint, Webcast, Zoom or Citrix or GoToMeeting, a website, a printed page, and a handwritten note, to name only a few. Tools are constantly being developed with new features, but they all must work within the limitations of their media richness level.

Uncertainty: The difference between what is known and the information required to adequately evaluate and act on a specific situation.

Index